Try It Like This Too

More Ways to Avoid the Hard Way

By

Jarrod Welsh

ISBN: 979-8-9854031-0-7

Cover design by Melissa Welsh, Cassidy Welsh
Library of Congress Control Number: 1-9538279881
Printed in the United States of America

Contents

FOREWORD

This is my second effort to help people and, if you're reading this, I hope I can help you. The main way I do this is by boiling everything down to its central idea, meaning, or cause to try and strip away all the extraneous garbage that tends to accumulate on/around the original concept. I have come to believe that this accumulation occurs both intentionally and unintentionally as well as innocently and maliciously. There are those who intentionally muddy the waters in the hopes of keeping others in the dark for their own gain. Some have the best intentions yet still seem to, however inadvertently, create a confusing or ambiguous situation. Analyzing these situations, and asking several questions, is the way to peel away the layers and get to the answer. It's so frustrating to see so much turmoil and strife in this nation based solely on the complicated and convoluted actions of our leaders. When I say "leaders" I don't just mean our government but leaders of any group or effort, be it race, religion, etc. Those "in charge" aim to pit groups against each other to ensure that A) they maintain their power and B) to preserve their idea of "order. The reason I put "in charge" in quotes is that, in actuality, "we the people" are in charge and it only takes us to come together to get results. Elections, prices, and power can be controlled by a concerted effort by "we the people". It's capitalism at its core, the consumer controls supply and demand. If the consumer no longer demands a product (or leader) then the manufacturer of that product loses money (or that elected official is voted out of office). But, as I alluded to in my previous book, complete solidarity is very difficult (almost impossible) to achieve.

Regardless of where you are in life this book should help you get better, or at least reflect on things forgotten, to reorient your life. Contact me with questions: jarrod@tryitlikethis.net.

Chapter 1

Social Media

When social media platforms began, they were revolutionary. They provided us a way to express our opinions to "the world", stay in contact with loved ones whom we rarely see, and even help our businesses. However, access to these "free" services has left us vulnerable to manipulation and exploitation. The same freedom that gave us a platform also provided others the means to express their opposing views which often leads to fruitless arguments between otherwise cordial acquaintances. I fell victim to this early on, being baited by subversives whose only intentions are to cause controversy to attract attention to their page. I found myself wasting time getting fired up about these ridiculous posts and feeling the uncontrollable urge to correct this misinformed soul who simply doesn't understand. What I should have realized is how futile the argument is because no one who posts is willing to change their point of view, including me. I felt foolish that I had wasted my time at all when I could have been doing more productive things. I have since deleted most of my "non-family" social media posts because of how pointless it all is. To be drawn in by someone whose sole purpose is to cause controversy is worse than the baiter's original drivel. So, if you feel that you are wasting time, effort, and emotion on responding to toxic people on the internet, the best option is to simply unfollow those who deal in tumult and flood your feeds with positive energy. After all, the goal in this life is to be happy and all your efforts should be to achieve that goal. Anything contrary to pursuing happiness is a wasted effort. You may be thinking "wait, I have friends who post both and I just ignore the negative things" and that is an option but, you have to ask yourself if the positive posts outweigh the negatives. If the answer is no, then you need to decide to sever ties with that person for your well-being. I had to make some of those tough decisions because, for some of the people I follow, the few positive things weren't worth the overwhelming negativity. Now when I access my social media, I only see positive things, like funny memes or pictures of my friends and family, and I have been much happier as a result.

This technique is also very helpful regarding the ads and suggestions you receive from your social media platforms. If you click certain things the algorithms used by the SM platforms will continue to send you similar items which could be good or bad depending on what you are clicking. If you click on links that upset you then you are at risk of receiving more of those types of links and becoming increasingly upset which is exactly the opposite of your goal. So, why do we do it? Because we think those links take us to "news" sites that will tell us the truth. This is seldom the case; we rarely ever read/hear the absolute truth. It is usually cloaked in biased verbiage and misleading connotation.

I can't imagine anyone believing anything they hear or read anymore. There is no absolute source of unbiased information anymore. Even our own eyes and ears betray us based on previous experiences but at least we receive the information firsthand and are able to fight back the urge to make a snap judgment and really assess what we've seen or heard.

The only way to truly combat the SM juggernauts are to manipulate them back. Use their own tools against them to disrupt their algorithms and control your fate. Don't allow yourself to be sucked into their suggestions. Look at everything through a lens of scrutiny and doubt and you'll never fall prey to their lies and manipulation. Better yet, as I said before, sanitize your feed so only positive, funny, or heartfelt information gets through. Use SM to cheer you up instead of allowing it to drag you down.

Honestly, SM robber barons don't care either way, they just want the ad revenue so, if you're going to use their apps, you might as well be happy doing it.

Chapter 2

Life Lessons

Taking Initiative

You don't need anyone's permission or guidance to do what you want. By that I mean you can pursue ANY endeavor you desire, don't wait for someone to tell you it's ok or look for any validation. When I was in special operations, we received specialized training that wasn't always offered or available to "conventional" units yet there were plenty of conventional guys who were better shots, in better shape, and better at the job simply because they took the initiative to go above and beyond what they were asked or what was expected of them. They had a personal drive to be better. They weren't forced to do these things, they did them on their own accord. The point is you can do anything you want. You don't need to be in a certain club or even accepted by certain people, you just need to take the initiative and accomplish your goals. Never let anyone tell you that you can't do something, find out for yourself. Revel in the fact that you're being called a "try hard" or "wannabe" because it means you are being noticed for your hard work. Those who condemn hard work are obstacles to bypass on your way to greatness. Truly successful people will recognize hard work and reward it.

This applies to all aspects of life whether it be taking out a full trash can or taking that Farsi class you've been putting off or going after your dream job. This is often said but it doesn't sink into many people: time doesn't stop, and procrastinating is a crime against yourself. You are your best advocate, no one will work harder for you than you.

The great part about all of this is that you are attaining skills and becoming a better person, which can be incredibly lucrative if you work hard enough. I say work hard but if you're doing something you love is it work? Become great and people will take notice. Heck, just become better than most and you'll do well.

But never rest on your laurels. Always strive to do, and be, better – those who rely on their past accomplishments for credibility are already dead.

Breaking Bad Habits

I'm sure it's been said before but, to break bad habits you must form new, preferably opposing, ones. The most egregious bad habit that comes to mind-affecting a lot of Americans is overeating. Most people who overeat do so because they lead a sedentary lifestyle and eating is easy when you're not moving. On the contrary, it's downright difficult to eat while moving – try jogging with a sandwich or biking with a bowl of soup. All kidding aside, if you want to break a habit you must engage in an activity that not only distracts you but prevents you from engaging in the bad one.

There is also something to be said about not having a choice being a good motivator. Aside from the fact that some poor behavior may result in your death, there are ways to limit your choices to choose poorly. Usually this means soliciting help from a friend or hiring someone to help. Either way, when you ask someone to help you stop something you take the burden of choosing out of your hands. Some don't have the ability to do it themselves, at first, but with help from someone else they will not only break their habit but will see how a motivated, strong willed, person acts and potentially change for the better.

For those who can't find a willing friend, or can't hire an assistant, getting creative is their only option. If you don't have the strength to stop your bad habit, then you will have to figure out ways of preventing it. The easiest one is to change your life pattern. Stop putting yourself in situations where you usually perform the bad habit. If that's not an option, then make doing the habit difficult. Implement barriers to the bad habit or do things that make the bad habit impossible later when you're weak. You can also make the bad habit undesirable by associating it (mentally or physically) with something that disgusts you. If you need specifics on your particular bad habit, send me an email to discuss: jarrod@tryitlikethis.net.

Another problem with breaking bad habits is ownership. No one is making you do the thing you need to quit. You must first accept that you have control over your actions and therefore can stop at any time. People say this is impossible, that the habit is too strong, but this is simply not true. We all have the inherent power to break bad habits, we simply must choose to do so.

These bad habits often prevent us from achieving our goals, but we disguise this behavior by saying, "things never go my way" or "things never work out for me". I believe, for the most part, we are the reason for success, or lack of success. Our actions, either out of ignorance or negligence, cause us to fall short of our goals. If you constantly find yourself blaming some cosmic entity for your shortcomings or failures, then it's time to reevaluate your life. You must pinpoint the occurrences, or trends, which take place, and reoccur, when your endeavors fail. Are you chronically late? Is your life overly hectic? Is your house/apartment in disarray? You must streamline, and unclutter, your life if you want true success. This doesn't just mean pick up your dirty laundry, it also means severing any toxic relationships you have, kicking any vices preventing you from ascending, etc. These distractions will prevent you from fully focusing on your goals thereby decreasing your chances of attaining them. Clearing away the extraneous obstructions from your life will leave you free to focus on what's important which is attaining happiness and "wealth". I put wealth in quotes because wealth means different things to different people. Like I've said before, you need only accumulate enough wealth to make you happy and for some that isn't as much as you think.

Speaking of making yourself happy, what is this obsession with ingesting drugs and alcohol? When I was in high school it was the thing to do, mainly because there was nothing else to do, or so we thought. There were plenty of things to do but the culture was that being "messed up" was cool and if you didn't at least drink you were lame. I had a good buddy who used to never drink and would always leave the parties at a decent hour. Everyone kinda gave him grief for that but he was actually the smartest of us all. Drank water while we were getting wasted. Went home and got some sleep while we were miserable the next day. Some say "well, he missed out on a good time" but I say he experienced the best of both – hung out with us then went home and got some rest. It's the same today, there's the old saying "poor guy doesn't drink, that's the best he's going to feel all day". This used to be funny but the more I thought about it the more it is just sad, that some people can't feel great without being inebriated. Yes, it was a joke told by a guy who is famous for being funny, but I believe some hold fast to this logic. Why not strive to feel good all the time through good mental and physical fitness? I stopped drinking alcohol and ingesting caffeine (for the most part) and I've never felt better in my life. I sleep better, wake refreshed, have energy, and generally am happy all day. Once you reach this point you won't believe you could have ever lived any other way.

I can't help but feel that most, if not all, people are manipulated by alcohol companies, television, movies, etc. to think that taking drugs and/or drinking alcohol are the only way to be happy and that a sober life is somehow less than or lame. This concept seems very odd to me, just as odd as how prevalent drinking and drugs are in our society and being under the influence is somehow the norm.

Sleeping and Your Health

Speaking of bad habits, one that many Americans can't seem to shake is not getting enough sleep. We're so preoccupied with minutiae like movies, tv, social media, "partying", etc. that we sabotage our lives by staying up too late and not allowing our body to receive the rest it needs. People say they can operate on fewer hours of sleep, but studies have shown that simply because you can function doesn't mean you are maximizing your potential. You've just grown accustomed to operating on that many hours, so it seems normal. If you were to get 8-10 hours a night you would feel more rested and able to accomplish so much more. Yes, sleeping for that long means altering your lifestyle a bit. If you have to get up early for work, you must go to bed earlier at night. It's not that bad to go to bed at 10 pm and wake up at 6 am, or whenever you need to, so you obtain 8 hours. Some say they can't just go to sleep, that they toss and turn, or their mind keeps them awake. To those people, I say evaluate your lifestyle. Are you exercising 30 min a day? Are you eating correctly? Are you drinking caffeine after midday? If you follow these suggestions, you should have no problem nodding off at night.

So many health problems can be solved by sleep. Not the least of which being weight control. So many health problems are attributed to obesity. Getting enough sleep allows your mind to be sharp to make good decisions (like not drinking the giant coffee milkshake). It also increases your metabolism because your body is not trying to conserve energy to expend during your exorbitant amount of "awake time". It'll feel comfortable shutting down earlier since it knows it'll be out for eight hours or more. If it thinks it's going to be up for 18-20 hours, it will need to slow its use of the available calories which means you burn less.

Another positive aspect of getting on a sleep schedule is that you'll find yourself waking just before your alarm because your body is anticipating it. Varying when you go to sleep and when you wake is hard on your body and isn't conducive to good health. Some would disagree and claim that they operate at a high (or higher) level when they get less sleep, but I would like to see those same people after a week or so of a solid 8-hour sleep schedule.

One caveat: there is something to be said about conditioning your mind and body to operate with small amounts of sleep. While you may not be operating at 100% you will be considerably more effective than those who are used to getting 8-

10 hours then suddenly have to operate with less. I believe it would be such a shock to their system that they would be less effective than those who have grown accustomed to it.

However, a person can grow as strong as they want and, if they were the type of person who has the discipline to eat correctly, get plenty of sleep, and exercise then they should have the ability to adapt to getting less sleep, less food, etc. Which is the point, grow stronger in your life so when you do experience adversity, you're strong enough to endure whatever it is. Facing adversity already "behind the power curve" is not optimal and will most likely result in failure. Be prepared.

Making Change

Too often people look at "the world" and worry that it is doomed but usually that outlook is a result of the overwhelming, and misleading, influence of social media. Most people need only look around their immediate area and they will see that not only is their immediate area not doomed, but it is actually pretty good. The level of "good" varies by neighborhood but a virtually universal truth is if the community works to improve their problems, they can normally make their neighborhood's well-being significantly better. Unfortunately, people equate their own issues with those of the world and feel helpless to the overwhelmingly "global" problems. The key is to think locally and act locally. By this I mean stop focusing on everyone else and focus on your immediate area. Gather like-minded people and create change in your section of the world. The reason I say this is if you don't have buy-in from the people you are trying to help it is very difficult to make the kind of changes necessary for success. If every street, neighborhood, and town took care of their own area, their problems would be less likely to remain unresolved. Too often people try to start too big and set goals like "ending world hunger" or "creating an equal educational opportunity for all children", etc. So, start in your own area and, once your issues have been resolved, start expanding your sphere of influence to other neighborhoods, sharing ideas, helping where you can so they can achieve what you have.

It seems like a pipe dream or futile, and it may be for some areas due to an overwhelmingly selfish or indolent populace, but for those who have the wherewithal to try, it can be done. Also, those at the highest levels of government are rarely concerned with real change, only the illusion of it, and they use the hard work of those at the lower levels to take credit for things like decreasing unemployment, better economy, etc. Perhaps after you help your area you could run for office at the municipal, state, or even federal level. We need people who are willing to sacrifice some of their time for the greater good. Whether it be sending an email or calling your congressperson, our "leaders" respond to concerned citizens because they know the citizens are their key to reelection and, if the word gets out that a politician isn't helping their constituents, it won't bode well for the incumbents come election time.

Making change can be hard because not everyone shares your views or desires. Others may not care, or they might actually want the complete opposite of what you're proposing. If it is an important issue, then you must be diligent and "work toward yes". Often, we try to progress our efforts by ensuring everything is perfect before we move to the next step. The phrase "perfect is the enemy of good" applies in some situations. By this I mean that you may have a very good solution to your issue, but it may not contain everything you want. If this is the case, you must evaluate the items that you are unable to include in the plan and decide if you can live without them. If they won't negatively affect the plan, then allow yourself to let them go in order to execute the plan. Often, we get bogged down with extraneous information when we should really be eliminating the trivialities to finish the project.

Finding a "mate"

Does it strike anyone else as odd that people say, "it's time for me to settle down" or "I need to find someone to marry"? Given the divorce rate in this country, this thought process seems counterintuitive (and a bit self-sabotaging). We've been so ingrained with the notion that we have to get married and have children that people rush into it and compromise with someone who they don't entirely love and, most importantly, don't love them. It's no wonder the success rate is so dismal, people aren't waiting to find the one for them, they're just "finding" someone to fill an imaginary, self-imposed requirement.

The key to a healthy relationship is being comfortable with being alone. If you are unable to exist without the company of others, you are setting yourself up for failure because your goal will be to find "someone" instead of "the one". Once you have become comfortable with yourself, you can then assess potential mates objectively without the fear of being alone clouding your judgement.

Being comfortable with being alone will also assist in making decisions that are in your best interest. If you find that you misjudged your selection you will be able to make a clean break without the underlying anxiety of being alone. I feel that a lot of people stay with the "wrong" person because they are afraid they won't find anyone else, but if they were comfortable with being alone, this reason wouldn't even enter into their decision-making process. They could make an honest assessment of their happiness, and to what level their current partner contributes to it. If their current partner is not contributing to, or actively working against, their happiness, they should have no problem breaking ties with that person.

Bear in mind that a relationship is work. You can't act however you want and expect the relationship to flourish. There must be changes, maybe large, maybe small, but they usually have to occur before a harmonious relationship can be achieved. This requires being self-aware as well as being "tuned in" to your partner. You must assess how your actions are affecting your partner and, if necessary, change.

When people think of change, they worry that they will no longer be who they are or that their partner is trying to make them into someone they either can't or don't want to be. Obviously, this is a possibility and if that is occurring then you need to re-assess your relationship. However, most of the changes are simply little "tweaks" that are necessary to ensure the idiosyncrasies you developed as a single person living alone don't slowly wear down your partner.

There are things we all do that affect our partner consciously and subconsciously that can slowly erode a relationship. We don't notice the resentment until it's too late because our partner is either trying to be strong and not let your quirks bother them or they don't realize they are being affected by them because only their subconscious mind is noticing them. This latter example can be difficult to fix given that neither party is aware of the negative characteristic. This can be solved with increased self-awareness. Periodic evaluation of your daily activities in an empathetic way can alert you to your potentially annoying actions. Simply evaluate your actions from your partner's, or children's, point of view and make an honest assessment about how your actions would make you feel if someone else was doing them. It could be as small as leaving the cap off the toothpaste or making too much noise while everyone's asleep and as large as blatant disregard for anyone else in the home. I think men struggle with this because we have an overwhelming desire to do what we want resulting in unintentional selfish behavior. Some men still feel that their partner is inferior resulting in a lack of caring and empathy, further resulting in their partner's misery.

Open conversation with your partner, both incoming and outgoing (the definition of communication), is crucial to solve this problem. You must be open, and strong enough, to accept constructive criticism. Your partner must also feel comfortable telling you how they feel. If every time they have an issue you bite their head off then they will be less apt to share with you in the future and will simply suffer in silence, thereby increasing their misery and resentment toward you which may ultimately result in a negative relationship outcome.

Just as your partner must be made to feel comfortable sharing with you, you must also express yourself in a way that can be received by your partner. If you are too overbearing or uncaring with your delivery then your partner may not feel secure being completely honest with you, resulting in you not being able to receive honest feedback while your partner suffers with an increasingly negative feeling toward you. The negative feeling doesn't have to be resentment, although that is common, it could be sadness, contempt, or fear. None of these are what you want your partner to feel toward you.

Some may think that appeasing their partner, or changing to make their partner comfortable with them, is a sign of weakness but a strong person takes responsibility for their actions and doesn't allow those actions to negatively affect others. It's very easy to barrel through life, steamrolling over weaker people, but it takes a strong person to control their actions and do what's right for those they care about. The alternative is just being a bully and we all know bullies are the epitome of weakness.

Pain

Pain is part of life. The more you try to avoid it, the harder it will be when you encounter it. It reminds me of a quote I saw on a locker in my team room years ago: ***"You must hurt to win. We are all fit and strong. The difference is your willingness to suffer."*** It was credited to the Mongol warlord, Yasotay. I love this quote because it illustrates just how people become successful through "pain". I put pain in quotes because it is such a relative term and often misconstrued as always bad or something to avoid. Suffering manifests itself in many ways. There is both mental and physical suffering and there are different degrees of suffering. But one thing is true: those who endure the suffering usually come out on top. On top of what, you ask? Whatever endeavor you have undertaken, voluntary or involuntary. I include "involuntary" as an endeavor you have undertaken because, like it or not, you are in it, and you might as well own it to ensure you don't let it own you.

Mental pain can occur in many different situations. Whether it's a job, a relationship, or an extreme hardship, do your best to face your pain. Avoid shying away from it, or avoiding it, because you want to form a protective barrier between you and the pain. Much like the callouses that form on a weightlifter's hands, building mental callouses can be beneficial to ease the pain, allowing you to focus on the issue and determine a solution. If you constantly avoid pain, when the pain does come (and it will) you'll be overwhelmed and succumb to it. Building a resistance to it will arm you with the ability to still feel the pain but not let it control you. Some are thinking, "I don't actively avoid pain, but I simply don't encounter much of it, if at all. Well, two things could be occurring: one, you are already strong and the pain you encounter doesn't affect you or two, you have a pretty good life and are not faced with much adversity. The latter example may seem optimal but, as I said, pain will eventually come, and one should prepare themselves for it. Perhaps searching for controlled, painful situations is in order? It might be as simple as getting involved with less fortunate people in your community or watching a documentary on an upsetting subject. The point is to seek out situations that are uncomfortable to expose yourself to the feeling of pain so you can, at least, recognize it to avoid being blindsided by "real" pain.

While mental pain is the most likely kind humans will endure, one must figure out how to endure physical pain as well.

Living a sedentary, "easy" life may seem ideal but it is only setting you up for failure. How many older people suffer daily pain due to their sedentary lifestyle when they were younger? We must challenge our bodies periodically to build up a resistance to pain. Building this resistance protects our body with natural armor to prepare us for painful situations in the future. This is where your "willingness to suffer" is tested. Are you willing to suffer the pain now to avoid a much greater pain later? If not, you may get a chance to experience an exponentially greater suffering as you get older. Suffering at a controlled, incremental, pace can build that natural armor to avoid the chronic, debilitating, pain some endure later in life.

I've discussed mental and physical pain as two separate things, but I want to stress that neither are mutually exclusive. Experiencing mental pain can result in physical ailments as physical pain can affect mental acuity. The good thing about this is you'll be building both sets of armor (mental and physical) during each bout of suffering.

This will not only arm you for negative efforts but also for positive ones that may not exactly be pleasant. There are many things that are great for us that require a certain amount of suffering. We must envision these efforts as what they are instead of what they feel like. Often times we dread the good things because they don't feel good while we do them but, after we're through we feel great. Just focus on that future feeling while conducting the adverse endeavor and it'll help you through the hardship. This "present pain" could be working late, or exercising, or an undesirable home chore and focusing on the "future reward" will make the suffering bearable. This is the goal, your willingness to suffer coupled with the ability to endure the suffering. Those who have not honed these skills are forced to live substandard lives and not ascend to a higher level.

You mustn't shy away from adversity. Allowing yourself to be coddled, or coddling others, does nothing to help you, or them, achieve ascension. Coddling only ill-prepares you, and/or those you coddle, for future hardships. Dealing with, and overcoming, hardships "real time" prepares you not only for that particular hardship in the future should it reoccur, but less severe ones as well for you will have that extremely adverse experience to compare to all others. If the current adversity doesn't measure up to the worst you've experienced, then you have armor against the lesser occurrence. If you experience adversity that is worse than anything you've suffered, you should *"count it all joy"* because *"ye have fallen into divers temptations"* and facing and overcoming this adversity will leave you stronger than you were before. Your armor will be stronger and your ability to cope with adversity will increase. This is something in which to revel as you continue your ascent to greatness.

This isn't to say you should be cruel. Causing, or experiencing, unnecessary suffering is to be avoided. Receiving enough negative input to receive the message is sufficient to learn. Anything past this point is futile and could result in a negative effect than which you intended.

Success

A quick note about "success". As I've said before, success is relative and is defined by you alone. No one else can tell you if you are successful or not, you make that determination based on the criteria you have created. Never let anyone else define what success means to you.

One of the best ways to be successful is to make a change in your life by surrounding yourself with people who either share your goals or have attained them already. Keep company with those who will lift you up, not bring you down. This isn't to say that you can't have friends that aren't "on your level" financially, socially, or even intellectually, but ensure that you maintain relationships with those who are successful, driven, and optimistic or you'll find yourself dropping down levels instead of ascending.

Just as hanging out with successful people will help you, hanging out with unsuccessful people will bring you down. I don't mean those that try and are unsuccessful, I mean those people in your life who don't share your definition of success. If you want something in your life and those around you are a distraction or detriment to you attaining it, you must seriously consider distancing yourself from them. They may mean a great deal to you but if they are a hinderance to your success you either need to minimize the time spent with them or bring them with you on your journey. Either way, don't let anyone hold you back from your goals. Some people are content with simply existing and have no desire to better themselves, which is perfectly fine because this is America, and we are all free to do what we want, but if those are not conducive to your desires then make the change and limit your time with those people.

One way we sabotage our success is by starting with the best intentions and then resenting them later. For instance, it is imperative to care for your present and future self simultaneously. By this I mean you can't, fully, sacrifice your present happiness for future success. Some have done this and have accumulated great wealth and success, but at what cost? I believe that there must be a balance, for the future is not guaranteed and this life is about being happy, both now and in the future.

So, to care for your future self, you must prepare in the present. Now, this can seem tedious if done in the wrong mindset due to the irrational resentment you may have for your future self. This is understandable because we don't often think of our future self as us. This is illustrated by how much we overeat, overdrink (or drink at all), use drugs, etc. If we truly thought of ourselves in both the past and present concurrently, we would attack the preparational tasks with vigor and joy because we know how much it will make us better in the future. Making lists, eating correctly, getting enough sleep, etc., are all mechanisms to assist in our ascension and our present self should take great solace in those efforts.

This isn't to say we should live in the moment as often as possible. We simply have to find that sweet spot where we take advantage of joyous moments in the present while keeping one eye on the possible future. But, just like everything, there are exceptions. Staying up late talking to that special someone knowing you have to work the next day, foregoing a chore to maximize time with your family, etc. The key is to prioritize the things in your life and own the decisions you make. If those decisions prove to be poor, then you must do what is necessary to make up for the lost time/opportunity. Never accept your shortfalls, work harder to overcome them.

"Complaining" vs. Correcting Wrongs

Sometimes there's a fine line between "complaining" and bringing injustice to light. If someone or something is infringing on your pursuit of happiness, then an injustice is transpiring. If you simply highlight an issue but do nothing to rectify it then you're simply complaining. However, if you actively pursue a solution to the issue then you are correcting wrongs. Sometimes it only takes exposing the issue to rectify it. Other times it takes hard work. If you aren't willing to put in the work to make change then you really don't have the right to complain about it. This could be as easy as writing a letter or making a phone call and it could be as hard as running for public office. You must be willing to take that next step if you want real change to occur.

Some think that the problem is so obvious that it will surely be remedied by someone else, but they don't realize that there's a good chance that the other people are thinking the same thing. This causes the problem to go unrectified. Don't hesitate to identify a problem to those who can make the change and, if they don't make the change, feel empowered to elevate the issue to someone who can resolve the matter.

Unfortunately, there are those who think highlighting any problem is complaining, regardless of the gravity of the issue. Some think that we should just "shut up and color", especially when the offender is a large corporation or entity that seems untouchable. Obviously, I disagree and think that the little guy pushing back against the big guy is the American way. We the people have the power to make change, regardless of who the change will affect. If someone, anyone, is a roadblock to your pursuit of happiness then it is your responsibility, and your right, to challenge them.

There is a fine line between complaining and correcting, but when the problem is negatively affecting you or someone else, you must have the courage to act. This entails doing what is necessary to help. Think if everyone did this, think of how many issues would be resolved.

Speaking of "putting in the work" and complaining, we often find ourselves complaining about the way we look or the way we feel when our fate truly rests solely in our hands.

Regardless of your "barriers" be they real or fabricated, physical or mental, you must find a way to overcome those barriers and put in the work. I should say, you must put in the work if you want to improve. Some have no desire to improve and are perfectly content with being overweight or weak and/or unhealthy and to them I say, good for you, no one is obligated to do anything. People will tell you what you should do (like I am) but, ultimately, the choice is yours but the decision to be unhealthy must be coupled with the feeling of contentment, not guilt. If you make "poor" choices and feel bad about them later, then finding out what you need to change is easy; this is the time to put in the work.

FITNESS

Take fitness, for instance, people make all kinds of excuses why they shouldn't workout when they should just shut up and do it. Don't have time? Can't go to the gym? Don't have the equipment, clothing, etc.? It doesn't matter. Body weight exercises can be done anywhere at any time. Stand in your living room and do lunges or squats or steam engines, or pushups, or burpees, or jumping jacks, or v-ups while watching TV. Put on a movie or show or record you like and get to work. These things will distract your mind from the discomfort of exercising – your mind is your biggest LIMFAC (limiting factor), taking it out of the equation will result in your body maximizing its full potential.

Exercise as much as you can at a time (a set) then rest for the shortest amount of time necessary to do another set. Do this until the show is over, or for 30 min, or until the end of the record, etc. Remember to keep going until it is difficult to do, then do a little more. That little more is the key to improvement. If you only do what is comfortable, you will only maintain what you have and, if you're overweight, this is not optimal. As you continue to give that extra little bit each night you will find that you can do more and more, and the improvement will come faster and faster, and you'll want to go even harder. Eventually you will change your mindset and adopt this new lifestyle full time and won't ever want to go back to the way it was.

Do this every night/morning/etc. Change the exercise every day or, do the same exercise if you're feeling strong or not sore. Yes, your newly worked muscles will be sore at first but that will subside the stronger you get.

If you live in an area with favorable weather, or if you don't mind being wet/cold/hot/etc., then go outside and do these things. Get some headphones and something that plays music and get busy. You can walk or run, you can find a patch of grass to do bodyweight exercises, etc. If there is a particular activity you enjoy (basketball, soccer, tennis, etc.) then do that instead. Fitness doesn't have to be bodyweight exercises or lifting weights at the gym. Staying fit can be accomplished by any means available. The key is to elevate your heart rate and challenge your muscles - however you do this doesn't matter.

Keep this routine up for a month or so and notice the results. Even if you still eat like crap, you will gain strength. Now, having said that, I highly recommend eating fewer calories and healthier food. This can be easily done with an app on your phone or a notebook. It'll be a little tedious at first, keeping track of calories and types of food, but eventually you'll get to the point where you'll know how much you should eat and when you're not doing the "right" things (i.e., what's best for your body).

Once you reach your goals you will only need to maintain that level of fitness, if you want to but, I think you'll find that, as you continue your rise to power, you'll want to keep challenging yourself. Either way, you'll be significantly healthier, and feel exponentially better, than you did before, which should be everyone's goal – to feel good all the time.

Stress

We all experience, carry, and deal with stress in different ways. Some go for a run, some punch a bag, some smash things, etc. Once people do those things, they feel better and are able to "de-stress" and face the issue with a clear head. But sometimes we are unable to accomplish our de-stress technique and we continue to pile on the stress until we are exhausted, irrational, or even sick. I submit to you that your "de-stress activity" isn't necessary. When you do your de-stressing activity, it isn't any different than if you did it when you were not stressed. Given this fact, simply think about the feeling of relief you achieve from doing your de-stressing activity and "jump" your mind to that place. You don't have to perform the physical task, only remember what it feels like when you do.

Now, this isn't to say that you should stop exercising, or even smash things if that's a hobby of yours, but don't be a slave to it. Don't allow the stress to build simply because you couldn't go for that run or punch a bag. Think of how those activities make you feel and adopt that feeling. We do this at other times when we think of something that makes us happy to avoid being upset, why can't we do it to alleviate stress?

Once you master this technique you might feel embarrassed that you once had to physically accomplish the task to reach the appropriate mental plane to relieve your stress. You'll be able to go directly to that place whenever you want, and you'll see your stress level decrease exponentially. After time you won't even have to think of the feeling, you'll just associate the feeling of stress with relief and get there immediately. This, coupled with my other techniques of being confident, prepared, and happy will assist in this effort.

Mental Visualization

A technique many people use to prepare for a task is Mental Visualization. For those who don't know, it's a method where you "visualize", or see, yourself doing the task in your mind, "watching" yourself go through every step pertaining to the task, over and over again. I used this task a great deal when I was in the military. There were many tasks we had to perform and, while we trained a great deal, there were some tasks that we were unable to replicate until we were in the situation. Conducting Mental Visualization allowed us to "practice" the task several times before execution.

Parachuting, for instance. We conducted "pre-jump" on the ground once prior to every jump but, as the missions grew more complex, the more practice was necessary, for me anyway. So, while we waited to board the aircraft, and onboard the aircraft ascending to jump altitude, I would run through what I was going to do in my head. I would visualize myself executing the procedures necessary for a successful jump. At the beginning of my career, I would run through these procedures multiple times prior to each jump. As my proficiency increased my need to visualize decreased but I always ran through the procedures in my head at least once every jump.

You might already do something like this in your daily life without realizing it. It's a very simple process but can be extremely helpful if you don't have the ability to practice the actual task before execution.

The technique is to make the visualization as real as possible, focusing on every detail as if you were physically performing the task. The more details you visualize the better. The goal is to be so absolutely prepared that performing the actual task is second nature. This "muscle memory" will allow you to focus on the unknowns that will inevitably occur during the task. If you are an expert at what you do know, you'll be in a better position to handle what you don't.

Labels

I never understood the infatuation with labels. Why do we have this burning desire to "belong" to something? I think you truly evolve when you can be comfortable with just being yourself and not striving to be called something or be part of a certain group. Not to say that being part of something isn't great sometimes but it shouldn't define you. I think that's how people paint themselves into corners.

I think the most grievous example is a political party. Once a person identifies themselves with a political party it leaves them very little wiggle room to deviate from the party line. Yes, people do disagree with their party, but they're then met with scrutiny and their loyalty is questioned. If you have no loyalty to any particular party, then you have no obligation to anyone. It allows you to be free to think how you want and choose whomever you want.

Political parties aren't the only labels holding us back as a society. The fabricated social construct of race is also a divisive tactic used to separate us to ensure we're never fully unified. It's telling when those who profit from keeping people separated say things like "racism is taught". It truly is but not only by bigoted parents, but also by those who accentuate it, or even still recognize it. All children are the same in the eyes of other children. Most kids already know not to judge another by their appearance, it's only when progressive adults expose them to the thought that they make the correlation.

I get it, putting ourselves and others in figurative boxes makes us feel better sometimes. It's scary when you don't know what to expect from someone, but I submit to you that simply because that person claims a certain label doesn't mean they will adhere to every aspect of it. They may claim to follow their group but deviate when necessary or convenient. It's a waste of time to categorize everyone. Instead, if you have a question or questions about particular subjects, simply ask and see where that person stands on that particular issue. It is very possible for you to respect a person who has wildly differing views from yours. Exposing those views instead of assuming them based on an affiliation is the only way to truly know where the person stands.

Self-Worth

I think we all go through a time when we feel someone else is "better" than us (whatever that means) or above us in some way. I have grown to a point where I don't feel that any person is "above" anyone else. There are definitely levels of readiness/kindness/success that others may have risen to that we strive to achieve but to say that any person deserves my obedience or respect simply for the position in which they currently are is preposterous and self-defeating. You have to get to a healthy point in your life where you recognize greatness and either know you can achieve the same greatness or accept your limitations while still being secure in yourself. Simply because a person has money or "power" (which is ultimately given to them by their "subordinates" and can be taken away just as quickly given the right set of circumstances) some feel they deserve a certain amount of respect or reverence. This happened a lot in the military. A person would "achieve" a certain rank or position and instead of exercising humility and grace they see it as something they were owed and "deserve". Not that we don't all deserve the success we achieve, but being placed in a position by someone else (which is how all positions are achieved, either by vote, necessity, or default) shouldn't make you feel powerful, it should make you feel humble that they are entrusting you with that job and are counting on you to perform it well and, ultimately, care for those for whom you have been put in charge.

This brings me back to those who "bow down" or "cower" before those who think they are "better" than them. If a person achieves success, they should be commended but they are still just people and should be treated accordingly. Recognize their efforts but draw the line at fawning/bowing/kissing a**. No one is important enough for you to devalue yourself. Be professional but stand tall and maintain your self-respect.

I think the worst example of this is how people swoon over entertainers (yes, professional athletes fall into this category). The least significant people on the planet are getting the majority of the attention. It's weird how people overly value the people whose sole job it is to gain the approval of the very people that overly value them. It's even stranger when those same entertainers feel they are better than those whose approval they need. It's even stranger still that "we" look down upon those who actually keep our society going, people we would actually need should they stop doing their job. Instead, people hold non-essential people in very high regard and discount those who are actually essential.

In the grand scheme of things, we are all equally important/non-important and we should act accordingly. Now, this doesn't mean to be rude, or prideful, or evil. It simply means that we all make mistakes, and we all have strengths. As long as someone is learning from their mistakes and attempting to hone their strengths, they can hold their head high. It's those who have a genuine disdain for others and refuse to live peacefully in society that deserve our rebuke.

When you get to the point where no insult or joke can affect you and you are able to dismiss it as quickly as you heard it then you have risen to the appropriate level. The fact that some can be taken down or negatively affected by another human's words/actions is laughable. There are those who claim to be "tough" yet allow another person to make them react simply by speaking. It makes no sense, unless you get to the root of the issue which is insecurity. That's probably why that person acts, dresses, speaks, the way they do, to make sure everyone knows how tough they are when the opposite is true. Yes, those people are probably "tough" with regard to physical fighting but is that really being tough? Isn't it tougher to rise above and ignore those who mean nothing? When a person's words can "hurt your feelings" then you haven't reached a high enough plane of existence. Choosing how you feel, regardless of the situation, is true strength, true power. If you can control your emotions and simply let things go, then you have truly ascended.

I mean, honestly, would you rather be the type of person who gets offended at every little thing? Seems exhausting. Or would you rather be like me, Teflon coated, someone who doesn't care what anyone else does or says as long as it doesn't affect me or my friends/family? Don't be a slave to someone's words. Rise above it and disregard them just as you should have disregarded their words. Or perhaps the "offensive" person is someone you have to see every day or is a friend or family. Maybe you can't remove yourself from the situation? In those cases, you either say something or grow thicker skin. By say something I mean tell the person how you feel. They may not intentionally want to offend, as I said, it may not be offensive to them as we all are different and have differing views of the world. Although, I feel it would be better to simply ignore because, if you make it known that the person is "offending" you then the offensive nature of the person may increase just to spite you. Never let on that someone is bothering you, especially if that is their goal. Giving someone the satisfaction of getting under your skin is never optimal. Now, I don't mean pretending that what they are saying doesn't bother you, I mean truly not caring and not letting what they say affect you. This will not be easy at first, but it will become easier the more you cease caring about what others think. To clarify, I don't mean do whatever you want, regardless of who you bother or hurt, I mean do the right thing at all times. If you do this then you will find it far easier to not care about what people say because you will know that what they say isn't true and that they are simply saying it as a futile attempt to offend, which is impossible because you have risen above petty things like that.

Chapter 3

Parenting

There are those who feel that having a child and putting up with all the difficulties associated with raising them, is a waste of their time. They feel that focusing on themselves and/or their spouse is the right path. To an extent they may be right, with regards to their life.

Then again, some parents believe they are righteous for "enduring" these "hardships" and they deserve sainthood for being so perseverant which always seemed weird to me because parents, normally, choose to have a child.

The truth is both are correct. There is no rhyme or reason to our existence and if one chooses not to have children then they are doing what they feel is best for them while those who have children are fulfilling their perceived life goals. However, there is something to be said about not knowing what you're missing. The small amounts of adversity a parent experiences are dwarfed by the overwhelming joy a parent receives from having children. Yes, there is much joy to be had being childless but we all, to some extent, usually experience that childless joy at some point in our lives. I think if those who are able to have children did, they would feel very differently about it.

Patience and Perseverance

As a parent, there will be times when you feel like your child will never pick up a task. Crawling, standing, walking, potty training, sometimes it feels like they will never get it but, each child will do these tasks (and others) when they are ready. This isn't to say you shouldn't practice, on the contrary, work with your child early and often and you'll find that they will eventually get it. This is where perseverance comes in. Never give up but also don't want it so bad that it consumes you. Just relax, keep plugging away "matter-of-factly" and you'll find that parenting will be much more enjoyable. Don't make the stakes so high on a lot of these things that you don't enjoy the teaching moments.

If your child has an accident or isn't getting a lesson you're teaching, conduct a quick evaluation of the situation to determine the level of concern you should have. Remember that things take time and there will most assuredly be "hiccups" in all of your teachings. Just take them in stride and know they won't last forever. Also, you have to determine if what happened is even a big deal. Is it a hassle for you to fix/cleanup/deal with? This is where a deep breath and some empathy can help you put things in perspective. Focusing on the child's feelings (having empathy) can alleviate a lot of frustration for you. This applies to all aspects of a child's behavior. Now, this isn't to say that you should coddle them but, staying calm and having some perspective will allow you to make a rational decision as opposed to blowing up and doing/saying something you'll regret.

Speaking of patience, learn to master it because parenting is hard if you don't. There will be times when you swear that your children are intentionally messing with you, but I assure you, this is not the case (when they're young, anyway – older kids will try to push your buttons). Some parents may have a natural knack for keeping their cool, but I would venture to say that it isn't common so, you'll need to find a calming routine to ensure you don't lose your cool and do something you'll regret which could be anything from yelling to something heinous like striking your child. This isn't to say that I condone or condemn "corporal" punishment, but if you do use it, it certainly isn't something to be administered when angry. There is too much of a risk of going too far. If you do choose to use it, ensure you are calm and dispense the punishment in a controlled manner. I would suggest this be the last resort due to the lasting effects it can have on a child.

Back to perseverance, do your best not to falter when it comes to your children's wellbeing. Of course you will but if you do stumble it should be slight next to the abundance of positive effort you put into their daily lives. I mean do everything you can. Volunteer at their school, run their Girl Scout meetings, coach their baseball team, etc. Check their homework every night. Carve out time to teach them a skill they won't learn in school. Do what it takes to make them as well rounded and prepared as possible for whatever they may encounter as an adult. This attention to detail will boost your child's chances of being great, which is the goal after all.

Childhood Obesity

There are parents who, inadvertently or deliberately, pass on their bad eating habits to their children. This is unfortunate and is due to the parent either not caring enough to stop the cycle or being unable to control their behavior, both resulting in an innocent victim suffering. These children are victims of their parents' actions and these children, like all other neglected/abused children, are innocent. I would venture to say that they are innocent until taught the proper way to eat and sometimes even beyond that due to the years of damage that has been ingrained into their character.

It's very easy to look at these children with contempt or disgust but that's a very immature way to see them. No, as with all abused children, obese children are victims that need to be rescued. But our country puts so much emphasis on food that it's no wonder children are overweight.

Large meals, with even larger portion sizes, at any and all occasions, special or otherwise, set us all up for failure. What is this infatuation with sitting down and eating three squares a day?

Some "Experts" have testified that 4-6 meals a day are optimal to not overfill your stomach and bog down your metabolism. Some also say it's better to eat smaller meals throughout the day to stoke the metabolism fire. I've also heard that fasting can be beneficial either to allow your body to use all of its calories or because humans were never meant to eat all day, that our ancestors hunted and/or gathered all day and ate when they found something. I've also heard that fasting increases our body's natural ability to fight disease, that this "hunger" stimulates our immune system to eradicate unknown threats before they manifest.

It's amazing how "wrong" we (humans) are sometimes. "Experts" claim one thing and then it's disproven years later. But is it? I don't believe there's a one size fits all remedy for all people, especially children. If your family is sitting down to a meal three times a day and your child is eating garbage, then don't be surprised when they gradually become unhealthy. I've had doctors tell me that when a child is hungry, they will eat so don't feel like you have to force them to eat. That being said, when they are ready to eat, you have to provide the right type of calories.

If you're having trouble with your child eating their vegetables for instance, then ensure you prepare and serve them first. After they get used to eating their vegetables first then you can start providing all of their food at the same time. I know this sounds tedious but, if they eat their favorite things first and drag their feet eating their least favorite then you're in for a contentious mealtime. However, if you only provide a healthy option then they have no other choice but to eat it. Now, I'm not talking about making them eat something they dislike, on the contrary, find as many healthy vegetables that they do like and put them on a rotation. Your child will eat the vegetables if there's nothing else. Then, once they've eaten the vegetables, feel free to serve something else that they like. My two-year-old loves peas but, if I put chicken, or hummus and naan, etc. in front of her, she is going to eat those first. But, if I just give her peas (or corn, or peppers) then she'll muck 'em down and sometimes not even want anything else. This is especially great at "dinner" time because I don't think it's healthy to eat a huge meal before bedtime and, since we've provided her with a healthy breakfast, healthy snacks, and a healthy lunch, there's nothing wrong with an all-veggie top off before bed.

Oh, and the only thing your kid should be drinking regularly is water and maybe milk. We give our kids soy milk because cow's milk doesn't agree with them (and one of them is vegan) but I drank cow's milk my entire childhood and I was pretty healthy, so I think, in moderation, milk is ok. Once in a while, I'll give my two-year-old chocolate soy milk and even apple juice on occasion. Trying to stick to a strict diet can backfire on you, especially if you don't expose your children to any "junk" food at all. If they ever discover it, and like it, they may go overboard and indulge too much. The best way to combat this is constant education. Tell them why the foods they eat are good for them. Tell them how each macronutrient makes them healthy and what happens if they eat too much sugar or trans-fat, etc. It's odd, before the internet when parents didn't have every single fact at their fingertips, there wasn't much of an obesity epidemic but, now that we can access a virtually infinite amount of information with a mouse click, our children are suffering. Lastly, stress to your children that food is fuel and not a pastime, that they shouldn't eat because the food tastes good but be happy that the food they are using for fuel doesn't taste bad. Stop associating activities with food. Don't "go out to eat", etc. (although I have to admit that going out to eat is one of my favorite things but only because I wasn't able to that often as a kid and now, I'm probably just overcompensating).

You are responsible for your child's health. If they are overweight, then you must do something to change this. No one else is responsible for them, it's up to you. The first thing you should do, however, is look inward. Are you healthy? Are you overweight? If you are setting a bad example, it will be difficult to make your child to act any other way. It all starts with us and acting correctly will significantly increase the chances of our children acting correctly.

Think About the Future

Always think about the repercussions of your actions, preferably before you execute those actions. Think about how they will affect your kids and their future selves. It's very hard to do in the moment if you're feeling lazy, or angry, or selfish and you try to justify what you're doing. It's not easy, and it won't always happen, but the more you do it the easier it will be. Even if you aren't able to do the right thing in the moment, you can still do some damage control by talking to your children about what happened and let them know that you made a mistake and that you're sorry and will try not to let it happen again. The worst thing you can do is blow it off and hope your children don't remember what happened but, if the incident is big enough, they'll have a hard time forgetting it. Even if they do consciously "forget", subconsciously they will remember, and it will affect them in the future. They may not even realize why they're behaving a certain way until much later in life, but the feeling will be there. They'll behave in a way that seems "normal", but it will be based on experience. This can also work the other way, the more positive things you do the better off your children will be, both consciously and subconsciously.

One of the biggest problems is a parent's ability, and willingness, to control their emotions. We tell our children to act correctly but then lose our cool and wonder why they follow suit.

As I've said before, if you want your child to act a certain way, you must first act that way.

Speaking of thinking about the future, if you have to do anything significant with your child, like name them for instance, take a second to think about it. Remember that this child has to live the rest of their life with that name and while you may think it's adorable, unique, and/or exquisite, it may be a royal pain in the neck for them later. I talk about being a selfless parent, this is one of those times when it is very important. Think about all the scenarios they will encounter and make an honest assessment of the ramifications of your actions.

On a slightly lighter note, speaking of "ramifications of actions", be very careful about doing things repeatedly or "habitually" because your kids will remember everything you do and if they love it you will have to do it every time. Whether it be a dance, song, saying, or other activity, if you do it more than once there's a good chance it'll become a family tradition. But who cares after all because your child's joy is something special and if you have to be a little silly or do something annoying to manifest that joy, so be it.

Along these same lines is daycare. Some say they don't want to work just to pay for daycare, but this only applies if you are a "good" parent. By this I mean are you the type of parent that is going to teach your child during the day or are you going to just let them play by themselves? Or will you play with them but not in a productive way? If the answer to any of these questions is no, then you should consider a good day care with structured learning time and actual "teachers". There's nothing wrong with working to pay for day care if it will assist your child's greatness. It's tough, though, to be honest with ourselves. Take my wife, for instance. She doesn't work during the day – in the evenings she's a personal trainer but during the day she "homeschools" our daughter. She has actual lessons and only allows educational programming. She takes our daughter to gymnastics, and music class, and soccer. She dedicates her day to the betterment of our child so her working just to send our child to daycare doesn't make sense in our situation. But, as I said, we have to be honest with ourselves. Will we do the same thing? Would it be better for you to go to work, get experience, interact with adults, while your child gets a quality education? Maybe.

Always be cognizant of the ramifications of your actions because they will have lasting effects on your children. Our goal is to create the best humans possible so ensure the majority of your parenting is focused on that goal. Not doing so will not only result in regret later on but also not setting your children up for the best life possible.

Divorce/Re-marriage

As someone who has experienced divorce, twice, my first bit of advice is to avoid it if possible. This isn't to say that you should stay in a relationship that doesn't make you happy, you shouldn't. However, if you have fallen out of love but there is a way to rekindle the relationship and be genuinely happy, then stick with it. Otherwise, make a clean and honest break. I want to emphasize "honest" because the shadier you are the worse your situation will be, both legally and spiritually. Legally because there are very few judges who look favorably on shady practices and will judge, and punish, accordingly. Spiritually because, regardless of what you believe, karma is real. It's either cosmic or manifested by our subconscious but it does factor into the situation. So, play it straight and don't be a jerk, especially if there are children involved. Let the other side be horrible and they will usually pay the price for it. Spiritually you'll be a lot better off acting honorably, even if you get raked over the coals.

Once the divorce is final you should take some time to get your life together before you seek another serious partner. There is much to do to get your life back on track and jumping into a new relationship is the worst thing you can do. You're in no condition mentally, physically, or spiritually to be a good partner to another person.

If you have kids, take some time to ensure your kids are squared away and not taking the breakup too hard. If you can swing it, get them some counseling to provide them an outlet for all the things they can't say to you or your ex. They will have a lot of questions and concerns and each age group will have a different set, but they should all be addressed before you attempt to move on with your personal life. The worst thing you can do is introduce them to someone new right away. This is bad for a bunch of reasons, not the least of which they may think you're trying to replace their other parent. Now, you may think this is a good idea depending on what your ex did to you, but it never is. The child doesn't see your ex the same way you do and, actually, the worse your ex was chances are your child will want them even more in their life. It doesn't make sense to us, but it makes perfect sense if you think about it, the "bad" parent is usually the one the child is trying hardest to please because they seldom get the attention, love, etc. they need from them. If you're in this situation, this will continue as they grow. You'll be the responsible parent, ensuring they get their homework done, eat correctly, do chores, get enough sleep, and behave while your ex neglects them. Your ex will appear to be the "cool" parent or the parent that allows them to do everything they're not supposed to. Your ex may do this out of spite, or they just might suck, but either way, it's going to be a struggle for you. The best thing to do is not take it personally, quell your anger, and do what's best for your kids. Even if they never appreciate you, you must ensure they grow up to be upstanding citizens. You can take solace in the fact that they will be squared away and have a good life, even if they never acknowledge that you got them there. Now, if the other parent sucked as a spouse but crushed as a parent then you're very fortunate and you should drop your grudge and revel in the fact that you both are doing right by your kids. It's a rare thing when two divorced people see eye to eye parentally so, if you have that relationship, work to preserve it.

While your child's wellbeing is your main priority, they will likely spend some time with their other parent which will allow you to pursue personal goals. This may be meeting someone else, getting in shape, or just taking time to process it all but, whatever you do, do not introduce a new "partner" to your kids until you are sure this person is a serious partner. There is nothing more confusing to a child than seeing their parent with someone new every couple of months, and it's not very healthy for you, either. If your ex is active in your child's life then you'll have ample opportunity to pursue a relationship but, when the kids are with you it's your time with them and it should be focused on them. There is nothing more selfish than a parent who shares custody yet still uses their time with their kids to pursue personal desires, especially when that involves having a "special" person over too early. Now, after you have been dating that person for a while and you think it's time to take it to the next level, you can slowly introduce the person into your activities with your children. You have to do this gradually and carefully. When I was dating my wife, I would tell her where we were going to be, and she would "run into us". This gave my kids a chance to talk to my wife and get to know her without them being overwhelmed or her being too invasive. This seemed to work pretty well for my younger daughter, but my older daughter was a little too savvy – she called BS on the "coincidental" encounters, but she was still cool about it because I didn't force my wife into their lives. They came to really love my wife and they still have a solid relationship with her to this day. Remember, while you aren't necessarily choosing a replacement for your ex, you are choosing a new parent for your children so choose wisely.

Speaking of "exes" don't be the kind of ex that takes your anger or resentment for your former spouse out on your children. This can take many forms but the most popular seems to be openly, and obviously, doing the opposite of what your ex says/does regarding the children.

Now, if you're doing the right thing by your kids and your ex is actively working against you then, by all means, keep it up. But, if you are the "bad" parent and your ex is trying to teach your kids to be upstanding citizens (be polite, eat right, exercise, etc.) and you are doing everything you can to disrupt that then you need to get your mind right and square yourself away. It isn't giving in to your ex to do the right thing for your children. Letting them eat what they want, go to bed when they want, and basically do what they want may win you some brownie points when they're young but eventually they will see through your BS and resent you for not being a good parent.

I just don't understand how a person can be so selfish that they intentionally sabotage their child's chances at greatness simply to "get back at" their ex. It speaks volumes about who they are as a person and probably why the relationship didn't work in the first place.

The best course of action, regardless of your "relationship" with your ex, is to be on the same page regarding your children. It may not be all the time but the more each home is the same the better for the children. Having to learn two different parenting styles, sets of rules, etc. is extremely tough on a child. It's especially hard when one parent scoffs at what the other parent does, and demeans the other parent, in front of the kids. This constant disruption makes it exponentially harder for the children to follow the rules at the diligent parent's house. The children feel like they are being overly disciplined in comparison to the other household when they are only experiencing normal parenting that would exist if the parents were still together. This type of "co-parenting" makes the children yearn for the lackadaisical parent's house because they feel like they are "free" when they are actually being neglected and set up for failure.

Alas, there isn't much a diligent parent can do because it's not illegal to be a bad parent and no one will get involved until it's too late, if at all. My advice is to stay diligent, always. It's very easy to simply give in and try to be the "fun" parent too but that does nothing for the children. Keep the children's wellbeing and success as your focus to ensure they receive as much "good" parenting as possible. Keep your cool, never take anything personally, and never get upset about what goes on at the other house. Simply do the right thing at your house and show your children how successful they can be by doing the right thing.

Something else to remember about getting remarried is that your new spouse may not have ever considered having their own children but changed their mind and decided they would like to conceive with you. This can be challenging because you have already been through it at least once and the newness and wonder may not be as abundant with you if it's there at all. This isn't to say that you're not excited, it's just not new to you so while you will still have that overwhelming feeling of joy one experiences from having a child, not everything will be exciting because you already know what to expect. However, you must try to remember what it felt like the first time so you can have those experiences with your current spouse. They have no idea what to expect, no matter how much you attempt to prepare them, and you owe it to them to match their excitement. Think back to the first time you realized you were going to be a parent, how excited and anxious you were, remember the uncertainty and apprehension. Have fun getting everything ready, don't just go through the motions because you've done it all before. Really embrace the experience.

A caveat, ensure you don't make the same mistakes you did the first time. Prepare your spouse for the times that aren't so fun (midnight feedings, no sleep, etc.) and ensure you have a plan to make those rough patches easier, if able. You really do have an advantage, don't squander it by "re-learning" everything.

Realistic Parenting

Too often I find myself holding my children to a higher standard than is probably necessary. Not to say that we shouldn't expect more from our kids, but we also have to remember that they're children and are always learning. We also have to remember that we were far from perfect as kids and, while we strive to make our children better than us, we should also take the "self-righteousness" out of our lessons to ensure we're not being disingenuous. I've found that it helps to give examples of how I fell short as a child and allow them to learn lessons vicariously instead of having to endure the negative experiences themselves. Not only does revealing your mistakes help your children now, but it will also help later when they find out you're not a superhero like they thought when they were a kid. Gradually learning this information will maintain a solid relationship built on honesty and trust.

Something else to remember, if you find yourself calling your kids "lazy" or think they are "messing with you", you must first look inward and own the fact that your children act as you do so while you're attempting to "on the spot correct" them, you must also change the way you behave. But again, you must also let them off the hook because children are rarely malicious in their behavior. Instead, realize that they don't really have the ability to think in those terms and, if they do seem to act that way, again, they are emulating you or someone else in their sphere of influence.

Another way you can help them is by making them do things on their own as soon as possible. Feeding themselves, putting their dishes in the sink/dishwasher, and cleaning up their toys are a couple of things they can start doing on their own way before you think their ready. You'll be surprised at how much they not only pick up but will want to do on their own. You can also encourage this autonomous behavior by storing their dishes/utensils and some of their food at their level so they can access them and start fixing their own breakfast, snack, etc.

We get so wrapped up in our schedule that we forget our primary purpose is to mold these little humans into something great. Providing the invaluable gift of autonomy will solidify a lasting foundation from which they can grow.

Another unrealistic parental behavior is putting much, if any, credence in their children's insults, barbs, and/or disrespect. Children don't normally know what they're saying, they are acting out of pure emotion and aren't weighing the gravity of their words/actions. Don't take anything they do or say personally. More often than not your children are simply trying to provoke a reaction, don't drop to their level and react. Keep calm and either discuss what they said and why or ignore it altogether. This can prove to be very difficult at first, but if you keep in mind that you're an adult who can't be provoked by childish insults and behavior, then it will be very easy to calmly deal with any situation.

Another reason to keep your cool in the situations mentioned above is to set a good example for your children. If you blow up at every little incident, then so will your kids. On the other hand, if you don't react enough then your children will run roughshod over you and continue to do so until you take a stand and refuse to accept their negative behavior.

Remember, whatever is "wrong" with a child is the parent's fault. The child either learns the poor behavior from the parent themselves or the environment in which the parent places the child. If the child is left with substandard adults, then the parent cannot blame the child for being substandard themselves. This is also true for a parent who does not parent with the child's best interest in mind.

I have always been fascinated with horrible parents who treat their kids poorly and wonder why their child acts poorly. It goes back to preparation for being a parent. There isn't any state or federally mandated class or training to be a parent, not that you could enforce it anyway. But it's kinda crazy that anyone can be a parent, regardless of their behavior. We're just setting up generations of people for failure by not, at least, making it available at no cost, if not making it, somewhat, mandatory; could prevent a lot of child services calls. Incidentally, this was one of my biggest complaints about the child services field, very little effort in the way of prevention. I always suggested ways of exposing people to sound parenting techniques, but it usually fell on deaf ears because "that's not what the agency does".

Another realistic parenting technique is not always giving your children a warning prior to a change in their environment. By this I mean that you don't always have to give them a 30-minute, 10-minute, 5-minute, etc., warning prior to bedtime, departure time, dinner time, etc. If you are constantly preparing them for something, then they will never be able to adapt should their situation change quickly or drastically. They will be so used to having someone prepare them for each change that they will have difficulty adjusting to the new set of circumstances. It doesn't have to be jarring or mean, but if it's time to go, or eat, etc., then they need to be able to drop what they're doing and get their shoes on, or get their PJs, on, or get their clothes off and get in the bath. This constant preparation isn't conducive to an adaptive child and isn't setting them up for success. Now, there is something to be said about letting them finish what they're doing or giving them a second to process the information, if they ask for it. This also teaches them that not every situation may be so important that they have to drop what they're doing. Teach them to communicate and identify when it's ok to ask for a little more time and when they need to move now. Obviously much of the responsibility for proper implementation of this technique falls on the parent. It is our responsibility to convey the proper information to allow the child to make an informed request/decision. Bring them up to the next level by setting them up for success. Doing these things will prepare your child for adulthood by giving them the tools to quickly adapt mentally to a change in their environment. It will teach them to instantly assess the situation in order to make an informed decision on how to act. This could apply to a fire alarm or car accident as well as an emergency work meeting or spur of the moment outing with friends. Bottomline, use your child's formative years to sharpen these skills so they are ready to use them when they reach adulthood.

Selflessness

I speak about it often, but parental selflessness is the key to a successful child. If you ever wonder if you're being selfish just stop and think about the situation. If you feel upset about having to do something for your child, you're being selfish. I'm not talking about things they can do for themselves but things that require your attention. Sometimes we get so wrapped up in our own stuff that we forget that we are responsible for every aspect of our child's lives. That feeling of annoyance, or sometimes anger, when our children ask us to help them while we're pre-occupied with something else is natural because humans are, at their core, self-serving life forms but, as a parent, you just have to take a beat to remember that your child is amazing and you want it to become infinitely greater than you so you drop what you're doing, within reason, and assist them. The task may be extremely menial or entirely insignificant, to you, but to your child, it is everything at that moment. Now, this isn't to say that you should ask "how high" every time they say jump but start wrapping your head around the fact that they are the priority. Some don't subscribe to this notion, that the children are as important as the parents. They feel the parents are in charge therefore superior, which is somewhat true, the "in charge" part, anyway. But as far as them being "superior" I disagree. I believe each member of the family is as important as the next and what they have to say should be heard with all the attention that an adult would receive. In doing this you not only instill a sense of self-esteem, but you also illustrate to them how much you love and respect them, a task some parents overlook.

Speaking of the way you talk to a child; I was having a debate with my oldest daughters recently about how I speak to my youngest. They were giving me grief because I speak to my youngest as I would anyone else. I don't "baby talk" her and I don't coddle her. I use language that she may not understand at first and, if she doesn't, I say it again in a way she can understand. My oldest daughters thought I was doing something wrong until I asked them how they became so articulate. They immediately understood. Infantilizing our children only prolongs their development and ascension to a higher plane. The more you speak to them normally the faster they will understand and hopefully respond in kind.

This also applies to everyday tasks like feeding themselves with a "regular" spoon, etc. People think they are "cheating" their children out of a childhood, but I submit that the kids don't care either way and treating children like "children" is mainly for the parents and their yearning for sentiment over practicality. Why not accelerate their development so they will be advanced when they enter adulthood? For instance, when a parent signs their child up for an activity like gymnastics, soccer, etc. and they allow their child to not pay attention to the class they think they are "letting their child be a child" but they are really setting their child up for failure. There is a time and place for "free play" and a structured activity that you are paying for isn't it. That's the time to hold your child accountable and get them used to following the rules when it's appropriate to do so. Parents who do not discipline their children in those settings are doing so for their own benefit, not their child's.

Again, waiting to teach your child the "right way" (read: the adult way) is doing them a disservice because they will now have to learn that lesson twice, if not more. Teaching them the correct way initially will ensure they stay ahead of the game, and their peers, and allow them to ascend higher and faster which will hopefully result in achieving success much sooner.

Praise/Excitement

Be very careful about how excited you get when your child does/wants to do something you love. An overabundance of joy and praise could have a negative effect on your child's desire to do that activity. For instance, I wrestled in high school and when my daughter expressed interest in wrestling I was overjoyed and overtly excited. I told her everything I knew about the sport as well as my experiences. I bought her all the best gear and actually was allowed to "coach" her on occasion. With the benefit of hindsight, I realize I sabotaged her wrestling career before it really began. She only wrestled for one season, and I know it was because of my involvement. As parents, we sometimes lose self-awareness and let our pride and happiness for our children overshadow them completely.

So, before you become "overly" supportive of your child's endeavors, make sure you have an accurate assessment of the relationship you have with your child, and temper your excitement accordingly. If you really want your child to excel you may have to back off a little (or, like in my case, a lot!).

Identifying Limitations

While I don't condone creating impossible situations for your child, I do support letting them work through an impossible issue instead of immediately stepping in to save them. I think it's important that they experience the feeling of helplessness firsthand to come to their own determination that a situation is impossible (or at least impossible for them) and either abandon the effort or seek help. Obviously, if they continue the exercise in futility, you may have to eventually step in and explain what is happening, but not too soon because we are all fallible and your child may actually find a solution that you weren't thinking of and teach you something. Either way, they will learn a valuable lesson about either perseverance or personal limitations.

Sometimes you have to actually show them that something can be done by either demonstrating it or guiding them through it. This may seem obvious, but some parents give up too early when just a little "nudge" could help the child surpass their initial apprehension. Obviously don't push them to the point where they become inconsolable or sustain an injury, but overcoming fear is about getting out of their comfort zone and realizing that their fears were unnecessary. Ensure that you always remain calm and supportive. It only takes one misstep to ruin the moment. Put yourself in their place and think of what it would be like to attempt the task, then think of what you would do and either explain that to the child or "assist" them through it.

"Overpraise"

Some think that "overpraising" your children is a bad idea because it may desensitize them to praise or make them overconfident, but I disagree. I think all accomplishments are worthy of praise, but the praise must be commensurate with the accomplishment. This not only lets your children know that they are doing well, but it also teaches them how to accept a compliment. Too often I've encountered people who are uncomfortable hearing praise. Probably because they weren't given a lot of it in their life. This could be for a number of reasons, but I feel that some were not given any validation by their parents. They could have also not accomplished much which makes the praise new and odd. Try to instill a sense of appreciation and humility by praising your children often.

In addition to teaching your children how to accept praise, commending them on their good behavior also teaches them that it is ok to give compliments and praise others and, if you do it correctly, when your child gives praise, it won't seem contrived and actually appear as genuine as their intentions. People are too quick to tear each other down nowadays, wouldn't it be refreshing if we could stop that behavior by instilling this ability in them?

Childproofing Your Home

Child proofing your home is important for a myriad of reasons, not the least of which being preservation of your sanity. Ensuring the area in which your child spends the majority of their time can seem daunting but is actually quite simple.

The best course of action when childproofing your house (or, at least the areas in which your child will spend most of their time) is to secure the exits. The easiest way to ensure your child cannot prematurely exit their designated confinement space is to install gates at all avenues of "escape", especially if those avenues lead to a flight of stairs. Gates can be expensive though so any obstacle the child cannot move, surmount, traverse, injure themselves on, crawl under or through is acceptable. Also, keep the doors to all accessible rooms closed to prevent any unauthorized visits.

Another "exit" that is often overlooked is a window. If your child has access to a window, you must ensure it is either closed and locked or make it inaccessible to your child. A screen will not protect your child from doing a header onto the sidewalk (some screens actually have a warning written on them) so ensure your child cannot tear, break, or push through the screens on windows.

Once the exits are secure you must scour the area for fragile, heavy, or otherwise dangerous items that could either harm or be harmed by your child. Think sharp corners on furniture, unsecured televisions, plants, tablecloths, etc. Either secure these items in a location they cannot be accessed by your child or remove them from the room completely. Preventing access could be as simple as erecting a barrier between your child and the item. The type of barrier depends on the age/agility/strength of your child and should be validated prior to allowing your child to roam "freely" about the room. Examples of barriers range from a piece of furniture that the child cannot move to a full size, extra-long, adjustable baby gate. I suggest a long (about sixteen feet), adjustable baby gate that can be extended to block one large area, or enclosed to create a secure area of about 19 sq. ft. The adjustable gate can also be configured into different shapes to block several different items. For instance, the gate could begin at the wall to block an outlet, then bent 90° to protect the side of your entertainment center, then bent another 90° to run in front of your entertainment center, then bent another 90° to secure the far side of the entertainment center. These barriers are especially important when preventing access to a fireplace, woodstove, etc. If you are unable, or unwilling, to block a piece of unstable furniture then you must secure it to the wall to prevent your child from pulling it onto themselves.

Speaking of outlets, denying access to electrical outlets is probably one of the most important precautions you can take. Most of the aforementioned "hazards" will result in some minor mischief, or a minor injury, but an unprotected outlet can prove fatal. You can pick up about twenty-four electrical outlet plug covers from the local retail store for about $5.

While you're at the retail store, pick up some child locks for your cabinets/drawers/stove/garbage can/etc. (basically anything you don't want your child accessing). They used to be a bit of a pain to install but you can grab some that are mounted by an adhesive preventing any need to break out the toolbox. Not all cabinets are absolutely necessary to secure, some parents allow their children to play with the pots and pans or plastic containers, but if you keep anything harmful or poisonous under the sink, you're going to want to lock it up to prevent any frantic calls to the Poison Control hotline (you do have that number handy, right?).

While your child's crib/bed doesn't seem like it needs to be "childproofed" a parent must take precautions to ensure the child is safe. For instance, if it's a crib, ensure it is free of all unnecessary bedding, stuffed animals, blankets, etc. These items can suffocate your child. As the child grows older and is able to rollover, a pillow and/or blanket can be introduced but keep the clutter to a minimum.

A baby monitor with video capability is also a very helpful item that allows you to keep an eye on your child from a remote location.

Also, make sure the mattress is low enough to prevent your child from scaling the rail and falling to the floor.

Baby monitors are not just for babies, they can also be helpful when you need to leave the properly child proofed room for an extended amount of time (e.g., to use the restroom, change over the laundry, etc.). This is especially important if you must leave your child unattended while they are eating – if you're not consistently checking on your child during a meal you will be unaware of any choking incident that occurs. The child will be unable to make noise to alert you to their situation, so it is imperative that you are either in the room or have a camera on your child any time they are eating.

While a child should never be left unattended outside, they may run in or out of the garage within your view so ensure you are either by their side to rescue them from an unanticipated descending garage door or periodically check the garage door sensors for operability.

Lastly, if you have blinds on your windows, you must ensure that the cords used to raise and lower the blinds are out of your child's reach. If your child gets tangled up in the cord, they could sustain a serious injury or die from strangulation.

While keeping your child safe is a full-time job, it doesn't have to be overwhelming or exhausting. Set you and your child up for success by ensuring the area in which your child is occupying is free of any and all hazards to give you the peace of mind and assurance that your child will be safe if you should need to take your eyes off of them for a few.

Preparation for the Future

This next part may seem like a bridge too far for families who are on a budget, but I submit to you that it is imperative if you want your child to be prepared for life. Extracurricular activities are no longer "nice to haves" but essential for your child's ascension. Some, if not all, of the activities I will mention can be taught by you or a relative for little to no cost if you have the skills.

But, if you don't, then you should budget your money so you can afford to pay for these skills.

The first extracurricular activity I highly recommend is some type of hand-to-hand combat. Whether it be jiujitsu, wrestling, kickboxing, or full up MMA, you must ensure that your child's first experience with having to fight off a would-be attacker isn't in a real-world scenario. They must know what it feels like to fight with all their might, so they know what it takes to repel an act of violence. You don't want your child to have to figure out how to get a potential date-rapist off them when it's happening in real-time. Even if you only wrestle with them in the living room, they need to know what it feels like for a grown man to grab hold of them and how much force and aggression it will take to stop the attack.

Another very important skill to learn is how to play a musical instrument. Studies have shown that learning how to read and play music assists in all aspects of learning and can contribute to educational success for your child. It enhances your child's ability to read, and more importantly, to retain what they've read.

It also allows your child to discover, and express, their creativity while challenging their mind.

The next endeavor may take some time to determine but getting your child into some type of athletic activity has multiple benefits to their well-being. It promotes a healthy lifestyle, exposes them to winning and losing, and depending on the sport, team building and camaraderie. I say this might take some time because we're never sure which sport/activity our children will like so we must expose them to as many as possible until one piques their interest.

This can start as early as someone will have them. At the time of this writing my two-year-old takes gymnastics twice a week and my wife hopes to get her into wrestling while I would like her to play baseball. Even if they seem interested in one thing, go ahead and expose them to other things to ensure they have been provided every opportunity. They very well may like something else even more. While focusing on one sport will hone a child's skill and provide them with every opportunity to possibly play the sport at the highest levels, this isn't realistic for most children and exposing a child to multiple disciplines will result in a well-rounded adult.

A physical activity that is imperative for your child to learn is how to swim. The ability to swim satisfies two life goals, being physically fit and being able to survive in the water.

Learning to swim should be one of the earliest skills your child masters. Whether you take them to the local pool, use your own, or visit the local lake/river/pond, it is absolutely imperative that your child learns to swim. You don't want to wait until they need that skill because by then it is usually too late. Even if you don't know how to swim, get them in the water and allow them to feel what it's like so they can get comfortable in that environment. This will also allow you to get comfortable in the water so you can eventually attain this skill. If you're unsure where to start simply look up videos or articles on the internet and use the techniques you find to get started. The biggest obstacle to swimming is fear. Once you realize that swimming is not a big deal, you'll be able to enjoy it. Email me if you have any questions or concerns, jarrod@tryitlikethis.net.

The "well-rounded" concept does not only apply to physical activity. Exposing your child to mental challenges and activities is also a must. The one that immediately comes to mind is speaking in public. I touch on this in my first book, but public speaking is a skill that can propel your child to a higher plane. Not only learning to speak in public but being comfortable doing it is a skill most never learn, let alone master. Exposing your child to public speaking at an early age will give them an advantage over their peers and save them a lot of grief in the future.

Once your child has become comfortable with public speaking, a logical next step is debate. Being able to conduct research and formulate a coherent opinion/argument on that research will prepare your child for all matter of encounters as an adult. Debate also prepares them to "think on their feet" when asked to provide an unprepared response to their argument. Being able to provide a lucid point and defend that point against rebuttal is a very rewarding talent.

I am a firm believer that children should learn as much as possible as early as possible because they don't have the fear that older kids and adults have. Enabling them to hone skills at a young age that they might normally fear if they were older allows them to bypass the anxiety and perform at their best. The key to all of this is your reaction, and description, of the tasks. If you preface anything with the inclination that they should fear it, they most certainly will. If you address every new task matter-of-factly, they will too. The biggest mistake a parent can make is projecting their fear, anxiety, etc. onto their child. It is imperative that we as parents mask our fear and exhibit calm when our children are experiencing unknowns. Give your kids a chance to use their inherent bravery.

There are many other avenues for your child to exercise their mind and, just as with the physical activity, you must expose them to as many as you can so they can decide which one they like. Don't let them stop at the first one, make them try as many things as possible, again, to ensure you're forming a well-rounded adult.

Now, preparation isn't always about what to give them but also what not to give, and how. Everyone knows that the more you say no to a child the more they want to do the thing you're denying. This aspect grows in size, scope, and danger as your child does and it's important to be able to say "no" to your child without fearing they will openly defy you and do it anyway.

I've found that honesty will nip most defiance in the bud. Explaining why they can't do something empowers them to take ownership of not doing something. The shining example that comes to mind is drugs and alcohol. Instead of threatening my kids (like I was) I flooded them with information about drugs and alcohol. The effects, the downsides, my past experiences. I showed them videos of people who used drugs and explained how achieving their goals would either be hindered, or impossible, by using.

You will need to take a different approach with small children who might now be able to grasp the concept of "why" but explain it anyway. Children respond to repetition and consistency. Eventually they will understand and that will save you from unnecessary battles at dinner/bath/bedtime. Telling your child the truth about why they need to sleep, eat their vegetables, and bathe will arm them with that knowledge and, before you know it, they will willingly do these things because they understand why. Never resort to "because I said so" unless it's absolutely necessary. It's the lazy way out and does nothing for your child's development. Yes, there will be occasions when you're too tired or they're too tired or there's an element of danger when "because I said so" is ok but don't make a habit of it. Focusing on your child's well-being and their future will assist in your diligence to do the right thing. If you resort to "because I said so" without providing any data on why they can't do a certain thing you run the risk of them developing an unhealthy want to do that thing and, as soon as they are able, they will do it, probably to excess. This could result in a drug habit, a weight problem, or crushing debt when an honest explanation could have prevented it from reaching those levels.

One last skill that I have yet to manage is the ability to type. For some reason I took two semesters of typing in high school and it was the one of the most important decisions I have made. With email being a significant, if not most important, form of communication in the world today, knowing how to type will ensure your child has a leg up on their peers. In addition to email, being able to type reports, research papers, etc. will assist them in college and beyond. It seems like an unnecessary skill, but I assure you, it has saved me hours of time.

Chapter 4

Guns

Gun Safety

All Americans are born with the right to keep and bear arms and I have no desire to curb or deny that right. That being said, I firmly believe it is utterly irresponsible for someone to sell someone else a firearm without ensuring they, at least, know the four rules of firearm safety:

1) Never point your firearm at anything you do not wish to destroy
2) Treat every firearm as if it is loaded
3) Know what is beyond your target before you fire
4) Keep your finger off the trigger until ready to fire

To allow a patron to leave a store with a deadly weapon without first imparting this basic knowledge is both irresponsible and dangerous. A firearm is like no other item a person can buy and should be treated accordingly. If people are aware and follow this guidance, they should be relatively safe if simply firing their weapon on the range.

Training

However, people do not limit their firearm use to the range, some buy a firearm for protection. The problem is that some of these people are not properly trained and are a hazard to themselves and others. As I've said before, you must "train like you fight" meaning that you need to train on the tasks you'll be executing in a "real world" situation. If you carry your firearm in your belt, then you need to practice drawing that weapon in training scenarios replicating real world situations. This is especially true for those of you who carry your firearm in your purse/handbag/backpack/etc. You don't want to have to draw your weapon for the first time in a real-world situation. You must practice accessing your bag, finding your firearm among the other items in the bag, etc. Conducting training will allow you to identify problems before you get into a defensive situation. You should try to find a specific place within the bag to store the weapon so you will be able to find it easily, quickly, and without looking. You want to ensure the firearm is clear of any other items in your bag so you don't inadvertently grab something as you draw.

You don't need to be at a firing range to conduct this training, you can practice drawing in your home. Ensure the firearm is unloaded then run through some drills to practice drawing the firearm from the bag. Conduct this training until the action is second nature or "muscle memory". Practice often to ensure you can do it without thinking should you find yourself in a "real world" situation.

This isn't to say you shouldn't visit the range as often as necessary to feel comfortable drawing and firing your weapon. When you're at the range ensure you are practicing with different target sizes and distances to increase your confidence level. Remember that smooth is fast and the less jerking, pulling, yanking you do with the firearm the better. You want to draw and fire with as little extra movement/time as possible while still maintaining accuracy. If you find your shot groups getting larger then you may want to slow down. If you're like me and just want to ensure you can hit a silhouette at 25 meters without any stray rounds, then you might not need to practice as much as someone who wants a shot group the size of a quarter. The important thing is to practice to ensure you can act quickly, smoothly, and deliberately.

Chapter 5

Education

"Summer School"

There is no reason for children to be out of school for three months. First of all, if your child doesn't continue "learning", or at least maintain what they learned the previous year, they can potentially lose 25-30 percent of the knowledge they acquired. This means that they will have to re-learn "old" information while trying to learn "new" material from the higher grade. If they were to go to school throughout the year they would maintain their knowledge while providing families a place for their children to be while parents are at work. It's lunacy for the education system in this country to assume that families can just find a place for their younger children to go during the summer. Nobody else gets summers off, why don't our educators understand that? This lack of understanding by our educators is not new as illustrated by early outs, teacher workdays, etc. The school day is geared toward teachers and administrators, not students and families. If the education system refuses to change to accommodate their "customer" then the government and businesses need to recognize that the schools do this and allow their employees to take time off to adjust to the family-unfriendly school schedule.

Contrarily, I do believe that a child doesn't have to be in school every day to be successful. My children are shining examples of that. If they need a day off, or if we have something we want to do during the school year, I don't find it to be troublesome to my kids. Obviously, it becomes incrementally difficult as the child grows older due to the unnecessarily complex subject matter and over-abundance of homework, but with proper preparation, and a little diligence, the child can easily persevere and be successful.

I believe that "educators" push the "in school every day" concept because, statistically, it may be correct but who compiled and presents those stats? From what area of the nation did they originate, etc. Those stats can't always be trusted, and you better believe they will be manipulated to illustrate that being at school every day is important and attendance needs to be as high as possible. Because if it were found that children didn't need to go as much during the week or that attendance levels were dropping then the money would cease and, ultimately, that's all that organizations like the department of education and the NEA care about.

The truth is it's about quality, not quantity. Focusing on the teachers and providing them with all possible tools to maximize their time with the students is key. Instead, we spend exorbitant amounts of money on frivolous "social" programs that don't guarantee results and are simply designed to make those in power look and feel good. It's all about money and making sure those in power are able to wield it without oversight from the people (i.e., the taxpayers).

Intelligence

It's an odd thing, intelligence. I listen to a lot of podcasts with "intelligent" people and they're always spouting off about how intelligent they are, and I wouldn't mention it if I didn't pick up some condescending overtones. As if people who haven't studied the same things as they have are somehow beneath them, intellectually. The truth is there are varying degrees and types of intelligence. "intellectuals" who claim to be cerebrally superior to others have simply studied different subjects than others. It seems like an odd thing to brag about and it's almost disingenuous to regurgitate things you've learned like you came up with them. Ok, you studied chemical engineering and I didn't, so you obviously know more about it than I but don't condescend as if you invented it. In the military, we called people like that "spotlighters" – people who drew attention to themselves because their self-esteem was so low. They wanted people to think they were squared away and, since they weren't, they had to draw attention to every accomplishment since they weren't very abundant.

There were also those who were totally squared away yet lacked the self-confidence to simply be good and not care if anyone else knew about it. It was unfortunate because people like these had much to offer but no one would listen to them because they were so blatantly spotlighting. They lacked humility and were seen as pretentious instead of proficient.

Back to defining intelligence, I know the dictionary definition but what IS it? Some think it hinges on how many books a person reads, and what kind. It also matters who wrote those books. I wonder how many theories and ideas have survived simply because a certain person wrote a book and "experts" thought it was good so everyone else did too. But who's to say those "experts" were right? Who's to say they aren't just perpetuating the same BS as the original guy? How often are people disputing textbooks, and who is ensuring they are accurate? It's more of a business than anything and I'm not so sure how good they need to be for a school to buy them (assuming the school has a choice). Are the books biased one way or the other? Are they skewed to fit a certain narrative? Bet on it. Which begs the question, who's to say the information people learn in college is the most accurate and non-biased information available? We just take for granted that the teachers/professors know what they're talking about and that whomever they learned from did as well. How are we to know? How many people have gone to school and learned about a certain subject only to find out that the real world doesn't operate that way? They find that the real world is not black and white and doesn't fit nicely into a curriculum and that

what they were taught often doesn't apply to real-world scenarios.

It's almost as if college is just a "gut check", a square to fill so a

company will feel more comfortable hiring you? I'm sure this is

less true in mathematical or history fields where the information

shouldn't change that much, but I'm not so sure about the more

abstract subjects.

School Districts

If I were lucky enough to be in charge of a school district

the first thing I would do was attempt to speak to each faculty

member in each of the schools in the district. Depending on the

district this may be a very arduous task, but I believe it is necessary

to get a feel for where everyone is educationally. I am a firm

believer that those on the front line have a pretty good idea of what

they need and how to execute the mission. While a superintendent

must make decisions at the strategic level, they can't do so in a

vacuum because those macro-level decisions ultimately affect

those at the micro-level. If I were in charge of the U.S.

Department of Education, I would ensure as much standardization as possible, not about testing, but what the "experts" think every kid should know at each level. I would gather all the data and ensure that what our children are learning is optimal for their success as an adult. I believe this data will come from the individual districts and the subject matter experts on the "front lines" of education. Too often administrators think they know better because they've "been there, done that" but things change, and skills atrophy the longer they are out of the job.

There shouldn't be any "bad schools" in a school district. Either they're all good or they're all bad. While the operation of each school should be standardized across the district, what will work for one school might not work for another. Given this information, slight modification should be made to ensure each student in every school is afforded the same educational opportunities.

This can be done in several ways but the most glaring problem I see in the "bad schools" is manpower. More teachers, more security, more faculty, more counselors, etc. Thriving schools don't need as much oversight and can function with what they have or less. "Problem" schools need more support to make up for whatever element is missing, or abundant, and causing the issues.

Misplaced Subject Matter Loyalty

One thing I've learned from being both a student and a parent is that each teacher and/or professor feels that their subject is the most important subject matter in each of their student's curriculum. While this is probably what we want in a teacher/professor, it's not always fair to the students. What I mean by this is sometimes an "over passionate" teacher assigns a little too much work to my kids as if they don't realize that they have other classes to worry about too. There have been many times that my children have been bogged down by an overzealous homework assignment resulting in them being unnecessarily stressed out because they have other homework assignments to complete. This goes back to my point about homework, it should be very rare and not very time consuming, so the kids have time for extracurricular activities in the evening. Again, I like that teachers are passionate about their subject but they also need to exercise some expectation management and realize that the children have other obligations besides the ones imposed in that particular teacher's class.

Unnecessarily Complex Subject Matter

Speaking of the subject matter being a burden, in my first book I discuss how there are some complex concepts that kids might not need to know until later, if at all. But, until this injustice is corrected, the least the teachers could do is explain how each of these concepts translates to real-world scenarios. This will help the students understand why they are being taught these concepts and it will also identify those concepts that have no explanation, or they have an explanation, but the explanation applies to so few people that the school district could seriously contemplate making that subject matter optional or eliminating it completely.

Mandatory Financial Education

I considered putting this section in the Presidential Goals chapter, and will implement this initiative if elected, but it definitely belongs here.

The amount of financial ignorance among our population is appalling. I myself didn't learn much about it until I was well into adulthood, and I believe most are in the same boat. There must be basic financial education classes taught in school to ensure kids are set up for success in the future. These topics should include, but are not limited to, balancing a budget, credit cards, loans, and investing. There should also be AP financial classes for those who are able to take them. These classes could include a stocks class that explains every aspect of investing from short selling to covered calls. Other classes could include real estate investing, crypto currency, and retirement funds.

I think the definition of "basic education" needs to be redefined to ensure we're teaching our children how to be great citizens, not simply great "students".

"Social Programs" in Schools

While I wholeheartedly agree with inclusivity in schools, I do not agree with spending precious funds on programs that are incapable of producing quantifiable results. Most of these social programs are designed to make everyone feel good or prevent school violence, etc. but what they really do is waste valuable, and sometimes priceless, resources like money and, most importantly, time.

All these programs "brief well" but, when put into practice, consistently fall short due to their inability to guarantee results. I mentioned this in TILT 1 but it bears repeating. These programs are based on theories and hopes, not facts. The money a school district receives is for the betterment of ALL students, not for a select few who feel unincluded or violent. There are positions in the school for students who fit those descriptions. The school counselors, deans of students, vice principal and principal to name a few. These personnel are trained to deal with these issues and are paid handsomely. To spend money on these programs when other, all inclusive, issues fester is a crime and those wasting these funds should be held accountable.

This is especially important in "poor" neighborhoods and districts where the funding isn't as abundant as other areas. These "underprivileged" districts need the funds to be spent prudently and wisely to ensure the students receive the education they deserve. However, administrators aren't concerned with students, only looking progressive and "hip" to show everyone they're toeing the party line and pushing the agenda/narrative. It's really sad that children are left behind due to the complacency of those charged with ensuring they aren't.

Physical Education, et al.

I've touched on this elsewhere but why isn't there more physical education in schools? I'm not just talking about dodgeball and four square, I'm talking about actual education that teaches students about living a healthy lifestyle. It seems like this aspect is glossed over at best when it should be a pillar of a child's education. We complain about health care in this country, yet we don't try to solve the root cause which is an abundance of ignorance regarding health and wellness. How much better off would our society be if our children had the foundational knowledge to be healthy? Instead of them having to struggle as an adult, they would already have the knowledge to make appropriate decisions about diet, exercise, sleep, etc. They wouldn't have to find out the hard way that drinking a bunch of caffeine will hinder sleep or that eating too much sugar can lead to obesity or worse. It already seems like our education system is just going through the motions, teaching the same subjects they always have because that's the way it has always been.

Along the same lines as physical activity in school, how is it that it costs hundreds of dollars for children to participate in school sports? When I played football and wrestled, I never had to pay a dime and I was given all the equipment I needed. Now kids must pay a fee up front to cover operating costs and they still must buy their uniform items. Maybe this fee is only for the "non-popular" or "non-money making" sports but what about those less fortunate families whose kids want to play those "non-popular" sports but can't afford the fee or uniform? School districts talk about inclusivity and equity, yet they deny "poor" families the chance to compete by not allotting funds for all sports equally.

Why don't we offer foreign languages in elementary school? Children are more apt to pick up on foreign language before age ten so why do we wait until high school? After eighteen the ability for a person to learn a foreign language decreases, or becomes more difficult, so why do we wait until children are reaching that threshold? Again, "we" are focusing too much on an old way of thinking when we should be aiming our sights higher, and broader. In addition to learning English, children in Japan learn how to cook and sew. Children can learn far more than they are given credit and we need to take advantage of that aptitude.

We spend so much time teaching children things they may not need that we don't have time to teach them basic life skills. Some might say there isn't enough time in the school day and to that I say extend the day and/or, as I said before, extend the school year to encompass the summer. It is an odd occurrence where I live right now, due to COVID, children have been distance learning, yet the days have been shorter. You would think that since the children didn't have to actually go into the school that the day could be longer, not too long as to preclude kids from engaging in extracurricular activities but at least the same length as they were before the pandemic. But my children's days are shorter, and their class load is much smaller. This doesn't make any sense. If a child only need open their computer to begin school, why would you allow them to start later and end earlier? Regardless, extending the school day/year allows for schools to incorporate the life skills I mentioned above.

You might say, well, those life skills are a parent's job! To this I say true, to a point. When you think about the normal family, children spend most of their day at school and only see their parents for a small amount of time each day. Couple this with parents lacking the proper skills and/or knowledge to teach these life skills, throw in those parents that couldn't be bothered to properly care for their children at all, let alone teach them anything, and you have exactly what we have right now. A perpetual group of high school grads who are ill prepared for adulthood.

In the current construct, teachers see our children more than we do, doesn't it make sense that the majority of life skills be taught at school? Then, as children grow older, they have that base knowledge and can decide if they would like to pursue STEAM educational paths or if they are content with other life goals.

The point is, there is no guarantee that America's children will learn anything if they aren't taught basic life skills in school. It is our duty as a country to ensure that children are prepared to be upstanding citizens first and rocket scientists later, if applicable.

College

Speaking of education, going to college has long been "the norm" for a lot of American families but is it really necessary? Are the colleges and universities still teaching what they used to? Or is it an indoctrination organization to generate more social justice warriors? It's just like everything, institutions of higher learning were probably established to teach those willing to learn advanced studies to prepare them for actual professions upon graduation. However, it seems they have strayed from that path and instead turned into establishments geared toward oppression rather than free thought.

One indicator that these institutions of higher learning have become less about education and more about changing students is the law that was passed to "protect" student's grades from their parents. The Family Educational Rights and Privacy Act or "FERPA" is a law that protects the privacy of student education records...even from those who pay the tuition. I was told by one university administrator that it is not the parent's business what their child's grades are, and that they are only privy to the cost of the tuition and how to pay it. This is absolute lunacy. A parent (or whomever is paying the tuition) no longer has the right to know if their student is failing and wasting thousands of dollars of their money. They just have to wait for four or more years until the students graduates, or not. This is just another example of an overcorrection of a "problem" that really wasn't a problem. I'm sure this law, like many bastardized laws, stemmed from an incident that was probably justified in that one unique instance which decayed into something unrecognizable from the original purpose of the law.

In addition to holding students accountable during their education process, each institution of higher learning should partner with businesses in their immediate area to allow for all students to at least visit, if not intern, at these establishments in order to see how their professions operate in the real world. Unfortunately, I fear that colleges and universities don't particularly care if their students are learning real world lessons, only that they pay their full tuition on time. The professors are usually those who did not venture out into the world to use the skills they learned in school but instead focused on teaching others what they've learned therefore not really knowing if what they've learned is valid or just what the previous professor learned from their professor, etc. Without real life experience to validate what is being taught, how can we possibly justify shelling out tens of thousands of dollars for this "education"? What assurances do we have that the professors are teaching the most current information? Yes, math and history are probably safe (although some are trying to change history), everything else has some sort of update or change that should probably be implemented into the curriculum. Regrettably, many of the professors have tenure which makes them virtually untouchable meaning they can do whatever they want with no repercussions. It's a crazy thing, an educator whose job it is to ensure their students receive the most relevant, and thorough, information has no obligation or incentive to do this. I'm sure I'm painting the profession with a broad brush but any professor who even acts this way occasionally is guilty of fraud and the wasting of their customer's money. People fail to realize that colleges are just that, businesses that have customers and the employees are the professors who are responsible for providing a service commensurate with the exorbitant fee being charged. That's why the military prefers instructors who are fresh from the battlefield to teach in their courses. These warriors have the most recent information and experience regarding their field and are best to teach those who will be in that situation in the future. Combat hardened veterans, regardless of their ability to teach, can always pass on lessons learned and current tactics, techniques, and procedures whereas even the best instructor will always fall short if they have not experienced, first-hand, what they're teaching.

Chapter 6

Military Experience

Optimal Lifestyle for the Military

This may not be a popular sentiment but it's absolutely true. Being single is the best way to serve in the military for a number of reasons but the most important one is being able to dedicate all your time to training and deployments. Granted, this may not apply to all career fields, but for warriors being single is the best way to serve.

It's virtually impossible to be a good spouse and/or father if you are training or deployed most of the time. Leaving town for weeks at a time for training or months, sometimes years, at a time for deployments is not conducive to a good home environment. Warriors do it but something is always lacking and it's usually the family. The other spouse and/or children are left to fend for themselves, and the warrior has little to no influence over the home life. This can lead to a resentful spouse or sad and/or undisciplined children. This isn't to say there aren't stellar spouses who work hard to pick up the slack of the warrior while they're gone but they still struggle and, no matter how stellar they are, the spouses still need their partner around to properly parent their children.

Additionally, a warrior may find it difficult to focus on training or combat if they are wondering how their family is doing back home. Some wonder if their spouse is struggling without them or if their children aren't be raised in the best way because their spouse doesn't have time to properly raise them because they are doing the work of two parents. Others wonder if their spouse is having an extramarital affair or spending all of the money but not paying the bills, etc. There are countless other scenarios that could distract a warrior that would be alleviated if they didn't have a family.

Warriors don't resent having a family, on the contrary, they usually love their family very much and is the main reason they fight. However, warriors are never more lethal than when they are single and have no outside distractions that may cause them to lose focus. Complete concentration is essential to success in training and on the battlefield and it's much easier to maintain this focus if you are single.

Relaxing

I'm not sure if anyone else feels this way but I inadvertently assess everything I do as if I'm in a life-or-death situation. It's a bit exhausting at times. Like, if I'm leaving the house in flip-flops I automatically think "what if I have to run for some reason?" Or, if I am getting dressed, I wonder if the clothes will somehow hinder my mobility. While the possibility of me going to a combat zone is less than zero, it doesn't stop me from assessing what might happen. It's a residual effect of decades of preparedness. While I don't think everyone should go to that extreme, I do think that a quick assessment of what the day holds is beneficial for all. It can save a lot of time and effort and hopefully make your day a little smoother.

Attitude

When you spend a significant amount of time in the combat arms profession, it's common to adopt an attitude of confidence some might misconstrue as arrogance. This can make life easier by preventing most people from giving you a hard time, but it can also prevent feedback and input from others. This attitude is not exclusive to the combat arms profession. Many others share this personality. If you come off as unwavering then people will be less apt to make suggestions or volunteer assistance because they feel it is futile due to your firm stance and perceived inability to compromise. If you don't realize you're being this way you need to verbalize often how open you are to suggestions and advice. This is also the case with those who, in addition to a firm and confident persona, have a dry sense of humor. It is often necessary to throw in a "just kidding" after your attempt at humor to ensure they don't take you seriously. I run into this issue often and the miscommunication creates a great deal of confusion and tumult.

Armed Conflict

There are those in the military who feel that U.S. casualties are an acceptable risk when engaging in armed conflict, but I disagree. I feel that our military leaders in the past were very irresponsible with the lives of their subordinates and that they simply weren't focused on the proper tactics. Now, I'm no War College graduate or great military mind but I don't see how ordering tens of thousands of your own troops to sacrifice their lives for a "strategic advantage" is a sound plan. I feel something else could have been done and the leaders at that time were focused on one thing (victory) more than another (keeping as many of their people alive as possible). George Patton said it best: "No bastard ever won a war by dying for his country. He won it by making the other poor dumb bastard die for his country." I fully support this logic. I think our current leaders do a great job of keeping to this ideal. Aside from the fact that these are American lives, and they should be protected at all costs, if our leaders throw caution to the wind and deplete our personnel then there will be no one to fight, hold ground, etc. I don't think we talk enough about how many needless deaths there have been in past wars. We glamorize it and say they're "heroes", which they are, but they are also victims of those "leaders" who failed to keep them alive. Now, I'm not so naïve as to think that no American lives will be lost in armed conflict but make no mistake, war is not a fair fight and, if it is, you need to reevaluate your tactics. The point is to win, not give the enemy a fighting chance. Optimally you would give the enemy no chance and defeat them before they have a chance to even fight. There was nothing better than surprising the enemy and taking them all without a shot. No, you don't blow much stuff up that way, but you also don't get blown up, which is the ultimate goal.

Speaking of making the other guy die for his country, I am a firm believer in being as honorable as possible but, if it comes down to my guys or theirs, I was always prepared to do whatever it took to save my guys' lives. After all, that's all you have out there on the battlefield, and I was never interested in giving the enemy a chance to fight back. Being nice doesn't win wars, being mean, and ruthless, does.

Embracing the Pain

There's a saying that bravery is being scared and doing the task anyway. Well, there's also something to be said about knowing something is going to be painful and doing it anyway. I think sometimes people don't want to admit that something sucks or is hard because it'll make them look weak. I disagree. There's nothing wrong with acknowledging something is, or is going to, be hard. It actually gets your mind right when you accept it and "embrace the pain". When you accept it, you take ownership of it and the pain becomes more manageable. I've said before to put your mind somewhere else to endure the pain but acknowledging that what you're doing sucks, and that very few people on the planet could do what you do, can help as well. Doing something you know is going to suck is true strength.

Diversity in the Military

There has recently been an effort in the military to make it more "diverse" and to spread "equity" throughout. But I submit to you that it has never been more conducive to the advancement of all people than it is right now. There are regulations, directives, and instructions that specifically prohibit any kind of discrimination based on any physical, mental, or spiritual characteristics. There are government sanctioned activities, functions, and events specifically designed to highlight virtually every race, creed, religion, sexual orientation, and gender. This behavior could be categorized as discrimination against those who do not fall into that particular category at that particular function or during that particular month.

Most evaluation methods are based on merit, not appearance as most boards are "paper only" meaning that each candidate for an award, etc. is submitted without a photo and without the candidates meeting the board in person.

Performance reports are completed based on the military members work, not their appearance and can be disputed if the member feels they are being discriminated against.

There are countless methods in place to prevent discrimination and afford each military member the opportunity to achieve whatever goals they desire if they meet the standards. Actually, the most squared away military member I've ever seen or met was a "person of color" and illustrated what can be done with determination and drive. He shattered stereotypes and rose through the ranks using all the opportunities the military provides everyone. He retired one of the most revered non-commissioned officers in the Air Force and is an example for us all. What he didn't do was take any handouts or special treatment. His success was a testament to what anyone can achieve in the military, regardless of what they look like.

The military is that one beacon of light that, I thought, rose above the progressive narrative that is plaguing the nation. However, it seems that some leaders have become "woke" and have turned the military into an institution not based on standards, but "feelings" and our warfighting capability will most likely suffer. People often forget that the military's specific function is to defend the U.S. People conform to the standards of the military, not the other way around. It's not designed that way to offend or exclude but to ensure success on the battlefield. I firmly believe that anyone should be allowed to do anything as long as they meet the standards, but it seems like some military leaders want to alter the standards to allow more people the "opportunity" to serve in certain capacities. This is a dangerous way to think. There have been countless people turned away from certain duty and/or the military based on their failure to meet the standard. Long before women wanted to be in all male career fields, men were failing to meet the standards and not allowed to join. The standards are there to ensure only qualified personnel are allowed to serve. The purpose of this is to ensure the best chance of victory on the battlefield. If we lower standards or give special treatment, for any reason, we are putting lives at risk.

There are many people who want to do many things but reality has a vote and simply because you "feel" you should be allowed to do something doesn't mean you can. Only hard work and determination to meet/exceed the standards should grant one access. Anything else is disrespectful to those who came before them and does a disservice to those who currently serve.

One last thing to think about. Our competitors/rivals/"enemies" don't care about people's feelings, they only care about victory. Yes, our compassion and humanity separate us from them but, while we lower our standards to coddle to feelings our rivals grow stronger.

Now, I realize that those who advocate for the lowering of standards aren't concerned about the future of the military, let alone the Country. They feel that America has always been grotesque and in need of a complete change. Unfortunately, the change they want is the opposite of what America is all about:

personal freedom, personal responsibility, and strength. Some would like nothing more for America to grow weaker and succumb to the growing inclination that we deserve to be taken down a peg or two.

Military Retirement

Can we stop pretending that a military pension is adequate for 20 years of military service? Maybe if you're a senior officer but for most other people in the military, a 20-year pension barely pays the rent. Yes, the amount increases the longer you stay in, but I submit to you that the life, and career, of a military member is significantly different than that of a civilian. Most of the retirees I know still work until the civilian retirement age. This doesn't seem right.

Maybe the retirement amount should be tailored to the career field. If your job is one that is physically demanding, or overly dangerous, then maybe you get paid more than others. If your job put you in harm's way, you should receive some compensation for your risk. This also makes sense since your options are probably going to be limited on the outside due to your skill set and the abuse you put on your body.

MDCOA

Another thing the military taught me was constantly thinking about worst case scenarios. In the military this is often referred to as "most dangerous course of action", but it doesn't have to be that grim, it simply means the worst possible outcome for your situation. Your "situation" could be that you need to attend several different things that occur on/about the same time, and you need to decide which event will be the least disadvantageous to your life if you miss some or all of it and which is the most important. Can you make them all for a short time and still be successful/polite? Can you miss one entirely without it being a detriment to your life? Will a phone call suffice? This technique can, and should, be applied to all aspect of your life. It doesn't take long and will become second nature the more you practice it.

Figuring out the MDCOA will not only help you make informed decisions in life, but it will also ensure that you are properly prepared in case the unthinkable does occur. One of the most harmful things to your wellbeing is being ill-prepared. Yes, it can be a tad time consuming at first but think of the time/money/happiness you'll save by just that little bit of preparation. Having some answers in your mental "hip pocket" can be the difference between success and failure.

For those who pride themselves on their adaptation skills, don't worry, you'll have plenty of opportunities to exercise those adaptation skills. As many have said before, no plan survives the first contact. There will always be a need to adapt and "tweak" your plan to ensure the greatest success.

Fight or Flight vs. Peace or War

I'm at the point in my life where I'm not ever "looking for a fight". This could mean many things, but in this instance, I mean actual fighting. I don't go looking for one and I try to avoid them at all costs. Some refer to this as the "fight or flight" response which is just a fancy name for being at peace until it's time for war.

Being at peace means that there isn't anything in this world that can rattle you to the point where you think you need to fight someone about it. There are so many situations I see/hear/experience where people want to fight someone else, mostly over petty things because they're too weak to rise above it and see the futility. I've mentioned this before but how weak do you have to be to allow another person to provoke an "involuntary" response from you?

Conversely, there are times when fighting or "war" is necessary. If someone is threatening your life or the lives of those you love then yes, going to "war' is acceptable. But, by going to war I mean just that. Using an amount of force that completely overwhelms those who mean you harm. I don't mean "put up your dukes", I mean grab a lug wrench or, better yet, a gun. The point of war is not just to win, but to win while making the enemy lose so bad that they are unable to fight anymore and must surrender. The same is true when defending yourself. You didn't ask for this to happen, your enemy chose to do this, you are simply responding to the aggression.

Of course, there are non-aggressive ways to deal with situations and I highly recommend using them to the fullest extent, but just as diplomacy fails in war, so can non-aggressive ways fail on "the street". Always have a couple of courses of action in mind in case things go south. Look for escape routes that will accommodate everyone you're trying to protect. It doesn't do your 3-year-old any good if your escape route is over the 10-foot, barbed wire fence. Your escape route may entail causing a distraction so your family can get away while you deal with the situation. It doesn't hurt to talk about these courses of action with those in your group to facilitate the execution of these COAs if necessary.

The bottom line is I try to stay "at peace" because allowing someone else to get me worked up to the point where I feel I need to "get physical" is weak. There are so many other ways to diffuse or ignore volatile situations that taking the "easy" way out and resorting to violence is actually the weakest choice, until an aggressor leaves you no choice. At that point you bring your full potential and use every possible resource at your disposal to "win the war".

Chapter 7

Personal Safety

Abduction

This may seem obvious, but I don't think many are aware of what to do if you find yourself in a situation where you are either being abducted or with someone you don't necessarily want to be with anymore. These are at opposite ends of the same situation and the concepts are the same, but the techniques are different. Your first move is to not put yourself in a potentially dangerous situation in the first place. Don't walk down dark alleys, go into a frat boy's bedroom, etc. Now, if you find yourself in an other than optimal situation you must prepare yourself mentally to do what's necessary to survive (whatever that means at the time). If you have to run, hide, or fight, visualize yourself doing it then execute. Don't hesitate because the best time to "escape" is at the beginning of the ordeal either due to ill-preparedness of the capture or your emotional investment in the situation. A captor's most vulnerable time is at the very beginning of the apprehension because there are too many variables that can thwart the abduction. Use this to your advantage and escape. You don't want to go to a second location because the attacker will most certainly have more resources there. Do what it takes to break free and run away.

Now, what I mean by "emotional investment" is when you are with someone and all seems very harmless and friendly, and you're having a great time, but something starts to change. The person you are with begins to act in a way that is unwelcome to you and you want to get out of the situation. Simply take a deep breath, visualize standing up and politely excusing yourself from the situation, then execute. Either tell them the truth or make up an excuse – or simply walk out. Whatever it takes for you to feel safe. The other person may not have had any nefarious intentions at all and simply liked you and wanted to pursue a physical relationship but, if that's not what you want then you are under no obligation to entertain the other person's notion. The way you handle the situation may need to be different depending on who the person is, but the goal is the same, and non-negotiable – get out of there.

Prevention

The best way to prevent occurrences like the one I mention above and others like mugging, rape, etc. are to prepare properly. One of the best ways to prepare is to be physically fit. Eat properly (email me if you don't know how: jarrod@tryitlikethis.net), get eight hours of sleep a night, and exercise. Doing these three things will keep you physically fit and mentally aware, two important weapons against any would-be assailants. Staying in a state of awareness that allows you to detect subtle details in your surroundings could be the difference between avoiding a situation and being right in the middle of one. The best way to get out of trouble is avoid it in the first place. However, there may be times where trouble is unavoidable, and that's where your health can help you. Being able to run away, or fight back enough to run away, could save your life. Obviously, taking some form of self-defense (jiu jitsu, mma, etc.) would help as well, but you want to ensure that your goal is not to practice fighting the assailant, but getting away. When confronted by an attacker, you are at a severe disadvantage because you don't know their intentions, plan, or possible help waiting in the wings. Your best bet is to disengage and seek safety. This begs the question though, how did you get into that situation in the first place? Again, not putting yourself in compromising positions is the best defense against trouble.

Speaking of prevention, this also applies to deescalating a situation as to not engage in hand-to-hand combat in "the street". If someone is being rude to you, your significant other, your children, or a friend, you have to be smart and not engage. First you must ask yourself if you're so weak that you allow someone else's words to affect your life. What do you care if some random idiot talks smack about you or your family/friends? That's exactly what they want, to get a reaction out of you. What if you do engage and you hurt the person and go to jail? Or, even worse, what if you are incapacitated and the assailant(s) go to work on your significant other or children? The best course of action is to deescalate and disengage. I equate everything to combat, and we never intentionally went into a situation where we thought the enemy had control of the battlefield or had the advantage. When you encounter a hostile in the street you don't know anything about them and must assume that if you engage that the situation will deteriorate. This will keep you focused on getting you and yours out of the situation quickly and safely.

All this being said, be prepared to fight. If you can carry a weapon, do so. Think of how you're going to use those weapons if the situation dictates. Always have a defensive strategy, even if it's very basic. Ensure it can be as easily revisited mentally as remembering your keys and wallet.

As with my combat analogy, always strive to have the upper hand. The street is no place for a "fair" fight. You didn't cause the situation, you're just dealing with it. You must do so in a manner that will either cause the other person to rethink their decision to engage or overwhelm them with superior "combat power" to ensure victory - victory in this case being you and yours getting out of the situation safely.

Chapter 8

Observations

"Saving the Planet"

I find it hilarious when people say they are trying to "save the planet" when what they mean (or should mean) is they're trying to save humanity. This planet has been around for billions of years and probably experienced many "global killer" events yet, here it is. Regardless of what we do to this planet, it will survive, we might not, but the Earth will still be here. Some think that humans have been here before, that humans evolve and then at some point get destroyed, and then the whole process starts over again. Heck, that might be the case because, given the infinite uncertainty of the universe, nothing can be ruled out.

Maybe the effort is futile (it kinda seems that way to me given the lack of effort by most of the world) and people who recycle, compost, and bring reusable bags to the grocery store are just spinning their wheels? The point is, people want to save themselves, not the planet. I have a feeling Earth will be around a lot longer than we will.

A better option is to start preparing for the worst. Scientists and engineers are working their tail off to stop something that seems inevitable, yet no one is working on any initiatives to protect us from the rising temperatures and sea levels. They simply, miraculously, want the whole world to stop causing harm to the environment. If we (the US) were smart, we would prepare our country for the worst and allow those who choose to trash the planet to suffer. We have to stop thinking globally and acting locally and start thinking and acting "locally". Trying to make the rest of the world like the U.S. is pointless and a waste of our resources and time. Just as countries like Iceland, Denmark, and Japan disregard others and focus on their country, we need to do the same. We need to modify the way we do things to ensure our citizens are protected from the inevitable climate change because regardless of the cause (natural or manmade) climate change happens. We need to figure out a way to sustain our water and food supply and protect our people from the elements. The Earth doesn't need us to protect it – on the contrary, it needs us to leave to thrive.

Apocalypse Prep

Apocalypses can come in all different shapes and sizes and, whether you think it'll be biblical, manmade, or simply a natural occurrence, the fact remains that you want to be ready. Now, many are saying "what?" to which I say, I hear ya. The word "apocalypse" has such cartoonish connotations that many of us don't take it seriously. However, prepping for one can save you some hassle if you do experience an event that may not necessarily eradicate humanity but could put a dent in the population in your immediate area. For instance, I live in Alaska where we have extremely cold temperatures, earthquakes, volcanoes, and animals that have humans in their food chain (and I don't mean the top). Preparing for the worst, even at the most basic level, can help you survive, and more importantly, bounce back, after the not-so-apocalyptic emergency occurs.

The first step in preparing for the worst is to get yourself in adequate shape. You don't have to have a six-pack but you need to eat your veggies, drink water, watch your sugar intake, and most importantly, exercise. Most people probably don't think about these lifestyle choices in this way, they do them because they want to feel good and live a long and happy life and this is perfectly fine. I, on the other hand, always think of worst-case scenarios and if I'm in a situation where I have to stay on the move or fight or hunt, I want to be in the kinda shape that would facilitate that. This is yet another reason not to use drugs/alcohol. Could you imagine being addicted to something and then one day it not being available? I stopped drinking caffeine, using nicotine, and drinking alcohol a long time ago, not for the reason I am discussing right now, but because I didn't see the point. Being prepared for a natural disaster is just a positive residual effect. If caffeine, nicotine, and alcohol become scarce and/or non-available, there are going to be some incapacitated people experiencing some unnecessary suffering. These situations don't have to be apocalyptic, they could be a power grid malfunctioning, or your home being destroyed by a wildfire/earthquake/flood/etc. The point is, overcome all addictions to avoid any suffering in the future. Just think about your family needing you but you can't act because you have a splitting headache and are nauseous from not being able to have your coffee, or dip, etc. This line of thinking may be odd, and possibly crazy, to most people but I think living your life free of as much weakness as possible is a good idea for emergency preparedness and daily life. Rising to a higher plane and restricting anything that may "control" you allows you to focus on the important things in life.

The Future

Does it seem like our country, more specifically our government, is just spinning its wheels? It doesn't seem like we've made much progress in the last couple of decades like we're just content with keeping the status quo and not improving the country. Our legislative branch is the worst offender with their frivolous hearings, failure to balance our budget and pass actual bills to assist the people they were elected to serve. They're more concerned with staying in their position, getting rich, and fighting with the other side. We all know the fighting is all for show and they are two sides of the same coin, but "we" just sit idly by and take their garbage. Maybe it's just all futile and "we" are too ignorant to know any better. I'll tell you who isn't spinning their wheels, infighting, and wasting time/money/effort – China. Our "leaders" fight continually and pass meaningless legislation while China invests in real estate around the globe, manipulates their currency, and screws with us. We're so shortsighted and myopic that we can't figure out how to take this country to the next level. I have to believe that our leaders just aren't good at what they do and can't make our country better. I believe they are so selfish that they would rather play politics than serve their country.

Who's to say that this country will be around in the next 100, 500, or 1000 years? I don't think anyone cares. I think "we" care about our immediate future and that's it. It's hard to think otherwise given the minimal effort "we" exert doing something about it. It really is amazing that we allow such complacent egotists to run our country. Or maybe we're the suckers who actually care for no reason. Maybe those who are selfish and only work to line their own pockets have it all figured out? While we get frustrated and complain, our legislators stay in power and make decisions, not for us but themselves. Their intentions are apparent due to the blatantly obvious partisan grandstanding we witness daily.

Speaking of the future, people say that young people don't know how to survive without technology. That they would be lost in an apocalypse or survival situation. This may be true but there is also something to be said about moving forward and progressing. "Living in the past" is also a detriment because you are doing nothing to move the species forward. Yes, the future has little to do with us once we're gone but those innovations that help our species could be mastered, and improved upon, while we're still here so we can also benefit from them.

Don't get me wrong, I am a firm believer of knowing basic survival skills but only living that way, and scoffing or disregarding innovation and technology, is an unintelligent way to live. Why wouldn't you want to be a master of your surroundings, not just the surroundings that may occur if technology suddenly goes away? There is nothing wrong with being good at both – in the military we would always train on our new piece of kit because it usually made us faster, better, and more lethal. However, we would also know the basics, the "non-electric" if you will, ways to operate. We had radios but also knew hand and arm signals, or a signal mirror, in case using a radio wasn't practical. We used our GPS but also knew how to use a map and compass. We used advanced optics on our weapons but also trained on iron sites in the event our optics failed. The point is, master the newest technology while honing the basics.

Misplaced Sympathy

After working in child protection for the state, I realized that many people have a lot of "misplaced sympathy" regarding the parents of abused children. I heard a celebrity talking about how broken the foster care system is, and he was right however, his solution was to just give the parent money instead of "wasting" money on child protection workers, paying foster parents, etc. His example was a mother who leaves her children alone at night to prostitute herself so she can get money to take care of them. He suggested just paying her money so she didn't have to sell her body, but the problem is we don't know the whole story and won't until there is an investigation. The mother may be on drugs or simply chose that profession because it's easier (and more lucrative) than finding a "real" job (although a lot of people suggest "sex work" is a real job but that's another debate for another time). The point is, unless someone finds out the root cause of the neglect, the problem will never be solved. It's telling that a celebrity, while having his heart in the right place, thinks throwing money at the problem will solve it.

Privilege

People often talk about privilege and who has it. Some claim a certain race has more privilege than another but that is a disingenuous argument and one, frankly, to divide us. The fact is that it isn't just one thing that gives you privilege, it's several things that everyone has to some degree or another.

Where you are born has much to do with your degree of privilege. No American can complain about not having privilege, not anymore. This country has reached the point where any person can achieve anything they want as long as they are willing to put forth the effort and have the talent (no amount of privilege will guarantee you a spot on a professional sports team). Yes, some have more privilege than others based on where they were born in America, who they were born to, etc. but this has nothing to do with any particular characteristic or trait, it's simply dumb luck. Some Americans complain about not having the same chances or opportunities as others and to this I say, correct, neither did I, and neither did a lot of people but just think if we had been born in an impoverished nation, or to a set of abusive/neglectful/or unintelligent parents. The situation would have been much worse. The point is that the only thing stopping you is you. If you try something and it fails, keep trying. No one can stop you from working, managing your money properly, accessing the internet from a public library, etc. The tools are there to be successful, you simply need to take advantage of them. Some might say these tools aren't available due to ignorance of their existence which may be true but, in the age of everyone owning a smartphone where all the world's information is at your fingertips, it just takes a bit of ambition to obtain the information you seek.

Now, this isn't to say that we shouldn't be working to improve the schools in poor neighborhoods. I think it's a crime that children are receiving substandard educations because of where they were born but there has to be some interest from the community which we rarely see. Personal responsibility is very important, and the less ownership impoverished people take over their situation the more likely they will stay in that situation. Regardless of your education level, all humans can feel pain and discomfort, and simply acknowledging, and disliking, those feelings should be enough of a catalyst to search for ways to stop them. If a person continues to endure hardships yet does nothing to remedy their situation then they may well be destined for that hardship. But, to blame others for their plight is not only wrong but futile. Normal people don't feel responsible for the indolence of others. They may feel compelled to help in some way but not responsible. Honestly, this is the reason I'm writing this book. I have often been in a position where I was not "comfortable", and I sought out ways to remedy it. I received very little help, if any on my journey, on the contrary, I have hit many roadblocks to success that I acknowledged and worked to bypass. We should all feel energized when we don't receive help from others, it should increase our desire to succeed on our own.

The bottom line, everyone enjoys some degree of privilege. Instead of complaining that you don't have the same privilege as others, use yours to make yourself great.

Role Models

Something that always struck me funny was the notion that a child has to see someone that looks like them succeed before they can succeed. This seems odd because a child doesn't see race unless they are brought up that way. Most children unencumbered by race speak by their parents/influencers just see a successful person and don't think it impossible for them to achieve the same success. A perfect example is the abundance of "white" kids who wear jerseys of their favorite "black" sports stars. They pretend to be them, emulate their techniques, and strive to be them. The same is true for other kids. Again, the only things holding them back are the racist adults in their lives which is an absolute crime.

A Bit About Race

Why is it that people feel they need to associate themselves with a race? It seems odd to identify with a made-up social construct, because when you do you equate yourself to every other person in that "race", regardless of how horrible they are. That's why you only hear fanatics associate themselves with, or take "pride" in, the "white" race. Because most "white" people don't see themselves as part of a large group or "race", they just exist as individuals. They don't take pride in the accomplishments of other "white" people, and they certainly don't take ownership of those "white" people who are horrible.

Racists like to lump people together and, unfortunately, when you associate yourself with a race you are saying everyone in that race is the same, when that couldn't be further from the truth. It's a funny concept to condemn those who lump people together for bad things yet lump those same people together for the good things. Are they all the same or not? I say not, good or bad. Simply because a person of a certain "race" does something commendable doesn't mean the entire race is commendable. Why draw attention to the race of the person making the accomplishment? "The first ____ person to do 'x'". Ok, so they have a certain appearance, what does that have to do with their accomplishment or the rest of their "race"? It really takes away from the individual, like it's not about them and what they did, but about everyone else who society says looks like them. Lumping people together for good things makes as much sense as lumping them together for the bad. Whether they are Nobel prize winners, robber barons, or drug dealers, they are individuals who only represent themselves.

Dividing us by our race is the way those in "power" attempt to control us. Most people buy into it. They identify with a certain race because someone a long time ago decided to group people together. Now people feel like it's their idea to be associated with a certain race when it's all a fabricated construct to keep people in metaphorical cages.

Race, at its core, is meant to divide. That's why it's so easy for those charlatans who make their money from racial strife to stoke the fires of racism instead of letting it go out so we can ascend to a higher level of existence.

The concept of "race" is so nebulous that people don't even know what term to use to describe people. Sometimes they use several different terms in the same sentence. It just seems very restricting to limit your loyalty and assistance to just one group of people. We're all individuals who should be striving to help everyone less fortunate than us, regardless of what they look like because, irrespective of what race-baiters and bigots say, we're all humans, equally deserving of life, liberty, and the pursuit of happiness. We're all a mix of several different backgrounds and shouldn't allow anyone to label us anything other than human. Labels are hindrances, roadblocks, and crutches. I'll never understand why someone would allow themselves to be labeled, let alone label themselves.

Also, how do people get away with being overtly racist? I don't mean what you think. I'm talking about when a person speaks in a certain voice, or someone draws a picture, etc. and another person automatically determines it racist without any overt reference to any specific race. The "woke" claims racism but doesn't that mean that they are racist for assuming it was about a certain race? It 100% does. People like that are the true racists, people who think certain people won't do well on the SATs, or can't figure out how to secure a bank loan, or vote because of their race. This behavior is so blatant and hypocritical, yet society gives these people a pass because "their heart's in the right place". Well, I say it isn't in the right place and it's those very people who are to blame for the perpetuation of racism in America. They feel that other races need their help to survive when the strong people of those races know that it is up to them to make change and up to them to take advantage of what America has provided for them. This isn't to say that other races haven't had their share of unimaginable hardships, but to say that people of today are comparable with their ancestors is to diminish, and disrespect, the lives and efforts of those ancestors. The pendulum has swung, and people being held back because of how they look is coming to an end. However, we must be careful that the pendulum doesn't swing so hard the other way that it breaks. Well, I guess we don't, it actually seems like the pendulum is stuck right now with the degree of overcorrection that is occurring today. It's not enough to fully accept those who do not look like you as equals, you must work hard for them, or you are labeled as a racist. Americans can no longer mind their own business if they choose, they must take up the cross and march with everyone or be held accountable as if they are the same as those who perpetrate racism. Since when did America become the land of "you must do something"? I thought it was the land of the free? There are those of us who speak out against injustice and do our part to help those in need, regardless of how they look, but that isn't good enough. Only sticking up for those who the radicals deem worthy is approved.

We're all people and we all need to look out for each other, regardless of how we look. The more we allow people to divide us, the more divided we'll become. There doesn't need to be a war, there doesn't even need to be a disagreement, there only need be a simple disregard. A disregard for the baiting, a disregard for the ignorance, and certainly a disregard for the hate.

Race should be stricken from every form, survey, poll, etc. Those demographics are only used to divide us and only benefit those who profit from that division. It's a way to control us by "proving" that a certain race is at an advantage or disadvantage or that a certain race feels a certain way about an issue. Some will say that is how those in power keep certain races down but that is mostly just rhetoric of those on the other side attempting to manipulate. If all races truly want equality, they must act equal and accept nothing less. This comes from individuals refusing to be categorized as anything other than human. We are all humans, and we should all be treated the same – perpetuating racism, positive and negative, only continues the lie that we are different simply because of how we look. Continually pointing out our differences only perpetuates divisiveness. Question the motives of those who benefit from this division.

"Pink Tax"

I often hear women complain about a "pink tax" meaning that manufacturers charge more for an item typically purchased by men but in a "woman's color", whatever that means. While I think this is an obvious ploy to exploit women, I also believe the "women's" items cost more because the manufacturer probably doesn't make as many, so they have to charge a higher price to make their money back.

It doesn't make any sense to buy the specialty item when the "regular" item is what's needed. Do women think they will be judged for using a "man's" item? I guess the same could be said about a man using a "woman's" item, but "women's" items are usually a modified version of the original and probably costs more. This is another one of those first world problems that plague our nation.

Traffic

Here's a situation: there are two slow drivers paralleling each other on the road so no one can pass, oblivious, or indifferent, to what they're doing. You follow a little too close to the one in the left lane, the fast/passing lane, to indicate that you would like to go a little faster than they are currently. Somehow you make it around the slow drivers only to just miss the light and have them come up beside you. As they're shooting you that look to say "what was your hurry? We both got here at the same time", do you think they realize it's their fault you didn't make the light and were unnecessarily delayed? Or do you think they're just as oblivious to that as they were to hindering your progress? Situations like these happen daily due to unobservant drivers. Just the other day I was on the highway and a vehicle was just cruising along in the left lane (a common occurrence in interior Alaska) and, as I passed this person on the right I observed that it was a young woman who was holding their phone in front of their face and had the audacity to shoot me a look like I was doing something wrong. This is the problem, people are not considerate, or even cognizant, of other drivers on the road, which is kind of a perfect analogy for the way a lot of humans behave.

Your Subconscious

Some people think that we make all our decisions with our conscious mind. That we are overtly in control of our every move and that no outside forces are at work. Some people think they are guided by an invisible force that helps them make choices. No one knows for sure, but I have a theory that our subconscious mind is constantly collecting input from the outside world and using that information to influence our decisions. I believe that we see and hear much more than we realize, and our subconscious brains put that information to use. We don't realize it, on the contrary, some of us think it is "the universe" showing us the way. Again, I have no way to know for sure aside from deep hypnosis that may unlock the very details to which I'm referring but I just have a hunch that I am being guided not by some unknown/unseen force but by my own subliminal mind, which is considerably, probably infinitely, more intelligent than I could ever be "awake". It really does make sense; the world is full of stimuli, and we really only "see" a small percentage of it. But our minds are soaking it up like a sponge. I reckon there are those who are substantially more in tune with their guiding intuitive mind, probably the most successful people in the world. It's like a sixth sense, a feeling that you're making a right or wrong decision and, the more we listen to that invisible guidance, the better off we'll be. This is especially important when attempting a task and it becomes increasingly difficult. You keep plugging away but are unable to figure out what to do, or you keep running into roadblocks, etc. I believe that your subconscious mind is running through scenarios of why it isn't a good idea, and it is slowing your cognition down to the point of being ineffective. This is when we need to take a step back and decide if the effort is sound or if we should abandon it for now, or completely. I'm sure there are some who waste a great deal of time trying to solve an "insolvable" problem (for them anyway) when they should take a beat to either reassess or seek assistance.

A Bit About Religion

I find it odd that people pray for things, as if God only grants prayers and doesn't do anything unless he hears a prayer, yet things continue to happen without a prayer to go with it. What about unanswered prayers? Some say it's "God's will", but if it's all "God's will" then aren't prayers futile? I mean, God is omniscient, so he knows what you want before you do so asking for something is futile because it'll either happen or it won't according to God's will. It seems very selfish to pray for anything other than forgiveness. I feel that we should all be thankful for what we have and sorry for what we've done. Anything else seems out of line. Do people really believe that God won't help them unless they pray for it? What about when they don't pray but something good happens to them? Was that God or just luck?

Again, regardless of what you believe, one should always be thankful for what they have and seek forgiveness for what they've done – if for no other reason than it's good for your well-being. Humility and grace are invaluable traits that will serve you well. Whether you believe in God, Allah, Buddha, or something/nothing else, having those traits will keep you focused. You're either serving God or your subconscious (or both) but both demand these attributes for inner peace. One must only forgo either, or both, for a period of time to feel that lack of balance and peace. Some may not admit it, but its unavoidable and they will continue to seek stimuli to mask the feeling. Instead, they should own it and make the decision to, and this may sound cheesy, find harmony.

Being Secure In Yourself

I speak about this in my first book but being secure with yourself, and not caring about what others think, is a superpower that can save you a great deal of grief and anxiety. Too often I see people deny themselves something that makes them happy because they feel someone else will frown upon it. Like, if they admit they saw a certain movie, or like a certain song, or conduct a certain activity, that it defines them.

In addition to being ashamed of one's actions, there is also a phenomenon of doing things simply to impress others or buying something with the sole purpose to impress. Spending money or acting a certain way simply to gain the attention of others is also weak. I don't understand it. How could a human hold another human is such high regard that they feel the need to "put on a show" in order to impress them? Granted, there are humans who I respect deeply but I've never felt compelled to be fake around them. I expect people to accept me for who I am just as I do them. Yes, there are times when I will sincerely and honestly change how or who I am based on the actions of others but that is different. This is making a choice to be better based on the stellar actions of another. Everyone should be doing this in order to mature as a society. Unfortunately, most only do things that are easy and that will gain them instant notoriety with very little effort. Then there are those who take the "I don't care what people think" to the extreme and actually become a detriment to themselves because, deep down, they really do care what people think but are powerless to do anything about it, so they develop their "I don't care" chip on their shoulder. This type of behavior is self-destructive and, if continued, will only result in pain – and not the good kind.

Remember, nothing defines you unless you let it. People will try to label you at every turn because it makes them feel better to make sure they know what kind of person they are talking to, so they know what to say and how to act. This seems weak to me, to have to define someone before you speak your mind. I guess if your goal is to manipulate that person into doing something for you or, say something favorable about you to someone else, you may feel compelled to mask your true self but, again, that seems very weak. Perhaps you should change your goals, or change yourself, so you don't have to maintain the charade?

Volunteer "Leaders"

Having children involved in extracurricular activities like club sports teams or Girl Scouts urges a parent to volunteer their time to help these organizations. Without volunteers, these organizations would be unable to operate thereby eliminating opportunities for kids. Many parents are more than willing to give up their free time for their children because we know that, without us, the organization would fail. Which brings me to the "leaders" of some of these organizations. Maybe it's just Alaska but I have had some very odd experiences with the "leaders" of the organizations for which I volunteer. I've found that the "leaders" see themselves as "the boss" and are strangely quick to berate volunteers. I've found myself "in charge" of a group of volunteers and never felt comfortable "ordering" them around because they are adult professionals who are helping out so the organization can operate. I feel that, regardless of their actions, the utmost respect and care should be taken when "leading" them. This is actually a good way to lead any group of people. If you respect and empower people, they will normally do as you ask. However, I've experienced "leaders" who feel their position in the organization authorizes them to treat their volunteer force as subordinates. I've even seen, and experienced, these leaders scolding and attempting to reprimand the volunteers. I never understood this. If a volunteer is not performing in the manner in which the organization requires, a leader must respectfully, calmly, and matter-of-factly explain the issue to the volunteer and ask them to stop the behavior, regardless of how belligerent or negligent the volunteer is. I've experienced volunteers blatantly disregarding their duties and had to ask them politely to stop doing it and thanking them for their service to the organization because, at the end of the day, we need them and if the "leaders" of the organization have a reputation of being confrontational, people will be less apt to volunteer. Yes, there is something to be said about a volunteer needing to perform if they're going to offer their help, but the bottom line is that they don't have to be there, and the organization needs them.

When I'm in a volunteer leadership position I feel compelled to thank people often for their assistance and I've found that people are receptive to this and are motivated to help even more. I've also seen "leaders" take volunteers for granted and "rule" as if the volunteers are their employees. Usually these overbearing "leaders" are people who have not experienced much "power" in their life and when they are allowed to be in positions of "power" it goes straight to their head. It's fascinating that they are completely unaware of their behavior and the detriment it has on the volunteer force.

What I have experienced is that the children for whom the organization was created are extremely grateful and have a certain degree of reverence toward the volunteers. I have also experienced athlete representatives inadvertently, but rightfully, convicting "leaders" by pointing out that the people the committee was denouncing were volunteers and they should be more receptive and understanding of a person giving up their free time to support the organization.

Food, Water, Shelter

Somebody once asked why food and water aren't free if humans absolutely need them to survive? I'll add shelter to that mix as well given the harsh nature of a lot of areas. It's a fair point, why aren't they free? Some may say it's the responsibility of those who made the human to provide the care for the human and, to some degree, that's true. But, what about extenuating circumstances? I realize there are in fact provisions for this very thing (food banks, welfare, etc.) but should it be more readily available and abundant?

What about easing the regulations on grocery stores, restaurants, etc. regarding when they have to dispose of their food? It seems very wasteful and wrong that a pound of food per person per day is wasted in this country. Bill Gates, or Elon Musk, or Jeff Bezos can't figure out how to link up people with that food? Too much trouble? Too much liability? Can't hungry people sign a waiver to absolve the food provider of all liability? They can, there's just no money in it. Maybe we can give food distributors tax breaks or other incentives to dispose of their food in a way that can be easily salvaged or, set up a separate area adjacent to their building that distributes food to the poor?

Internet Empowerment of the "Little Guy"

I listen to several podcasts that have celebrities as guests and a lot of them have celebrities as hosts and I always get a kick out of how they scoff at "internet Stars". They are so distraught over the fact that a kid being goofy on YouTube can make millions while they are still grinding it out in comedy clubs or on television commercial auditions. They hate it that "normal" people are getting recognized for being funny when, in actuality, there are countless funny people in this world, many times more talented and funnier than the so called "celebrities". Fame used to be all about right place right time and/or quid pro quo. Now people are able to showcase their talents directly to America/The World, without having to jump through a bunch of hoops for, or wait to be discovered by, a handful of "gatekeepers". I've heard so many old, salty, celebrities complain that these "internet stars" didn't "pay their dues" like they did and don't "deserve" the fame and, most importantly to most of them, the money. I say, good for the "little guy".

For too long those at "the top" have determined who does what in this country and the "Little Guy" (read: everyday Americans) are starting to fight back. They are not only making themselves known in the entertainment world but in other realms as well. For instance, take the most recent example of Reddit users fighting back against wall street by stopping the short sell of Gamestop. Regular people doing what billion-dollar hedge funds have been doing for years, and it was not received well. How dare these "peons" affect the financial innerworkings of millionaires and billionaires?!! The audacity!!

Well, I personally love it. It illustrates how people can work together if they want to. It shows the true "power of the people". This same power can be wielded to control the government, as the Founding Fathers intended. As I've stated before, people demand term limits but only need to force that issue with their votes. Our "leaders" could be held accountable for their actions with the solidarity of the Nation.

Perhaps this new wave of unity will grow. Perhaps we will see the majority of us in the middle band together and defy the two-party system and vote for a third party. I know, the past has not boded well for a third-party candidate but only because people have been skeptical. Or maybe there hasn't been a candidate worthy of this powerful, unified vote. It just takes the power of the American people to take back control of our government from the biased and Un-American Democrat and Republican parties who each have one, shared goal…to be in power.

Immigration and Business

The point of a business is to make money. It's simple; most businesses will do whatever they can to make as much money as possible. That's how this country became so great so fast – blind ambition, greed and blood. Is it fair? No. Most things in life aren't. There are a lot of things that "should" be, according to our own morals and values – unfortunately, everyone doesn't share the same morals and values.

For instance, if you prevent companies from hiring "illegals", some will either fold because they can't afford to pay an honest wage or, if they have the means, they will move their operation to the cheap labor (overseas). Although most companies are probably concerned about the work ethic of their employees, I would venture to say not nearly as much as the cost to employ them. That's the attractive thing about the areas they choose – cheap labor is abundant. So, instead of "illegals" we make them "documented workers" by fingerprinting them, taking their picture, and giving them some sort of ID card with a number on it like a social security number so they can pay taxes. They won't get to vote until they become an actual citizen but, as long as they pay taxes, they'll be able to enjoy the benefits of those tax dollars.

To clarify, I certainly don't condone illegals, regardless of how honest and hardworking they are. Those to which I was referring are people already in the U.S. I've said it many times, the issue isn't the guy who wants to earn an honest living and send money back home - it's the sponges, criminals and terrorists that concern me. We must increase our border presence and stop everyone from illegally entering the U.S. to ensure the bad guys don't get through. If the good guys want in bad enough, they will take the proper steps to enter "legally". If the bad guys take the same steps, then they will be documented and in the system and can be tracked it they choose to continue their bad behavior.

Documenting, and taxing, illegals would also help the school systems as there are plenty of children of illegal immigrants taking advantage of the U.S. education system, yet their parents are not paying any taxes to support the schools. This creates a massive burden on the school district. I agree that all children should have an education (it would help our society exponentially) however, our country/government can't figure out how to effectively run an education system. If "we" focus significantly more effort (and money) on the education of our nation's children, we could probably handle the extra illegals. But with low teacher's salaries, growing class sizes and dwindling/mismanaged budgets, we're barely getting by as it is. If illegals became documented and paid taxes, a large portion of this burden would be alleviated.

This is where the government comes in; if U.S. laws made it more attractive and lucrative to run a business here then there might be fewer issues. Business is, too often, treated like the bad guy, or the answer to balancing the budget (taxes), instead of the backbone of this country.

Normalization

People often wonder how atrocities occur, but I believe that they occur just as anything does, through the normalization of such acts. Everyone starts at a baseline and anything that is below that baseline is considered unacceptable. But what if your baseline is much higher than someone else's? Then the things you see those living below your baseline do are considered unacceptable. Just as those who live above your baseline considered some of your actions unacceptable. Well, the same can be said for those who live well below what you may consider a "normal" baseline. Take North Korea, for example. Famous defector, Yeonmi Park, claims that dead bodies are so abundant and prevalent that it is "normal" to see them. In the street, in the bus station, behind the hospital, etc. This kind of normalcy would abhor most people but, to them, having always lived in that environment, it is completely normal. This kind of behavior explains why we continue to eat excessively or drink alcohol/do drugs, because we have been doing it for so long that it has become "the norm" and no longer seems odd or wrong. Some say it is difficult to identify these "norms" because they are so ingrained, but I believe that we don't want to acknowledge them because that would mean we have to change. Food is my problem. I know I'm supposed to use food as fuel and only eat when I'm hungry, yet I continue to binge eat. It could stem from a few things, maybe starving myself during high school wrestling or maybe not having abundant food as a child? Maybe I just have an obsessive personality where I have to do the thing I like to excess. Whatever the reason, it only took me to be honest with myself to identify the issue. Now, this isn't to say the solution is going to be easy, but you can't solve a problem if you don't know what it is, and honestly evaluating yourself is the first step at a solution. Unfortunately, there are many people who never come to this realization, or at least never admit it, and they continue to ingest their "vice" (food/drugs/alcohol) until they have reached an unhealthy level. They can't remember how they got there because it happened slowly. This is how heinous activities occur. It is often said that the holocaust didn't happen overnight and that by the time it got to that point it was too late. No one can imagine that this could happen but, if the severity of the issue is gradually elevated then it seems "normal" because a person is exposed to it over time and only at "tolerable" levels.

The key to stopping gradual changes like these are action by all. It's not enough for a few motivated people to act, it takes many. Too often we rely on a few to help "us" stop, or get out of, situations instead of us all being proactive in the beginning. Those "in power" run roughshod over the people of this country and it's mainly due to inaction or indifference. People are content in their own lives as long as they aren't being negatively affected by other people's plight. Unfortunately, those negatively affected are usually powerless against the "system" because they either don't have the money or time, or both, to properly remedy the situation. Additionally, as previously stated, they don't have the support of others because it isn't directly affecting those others. Local governments are supposed to help those in these situations, but far too often, the problems of the people don't align with the priorities of the governments, or the governments are ignorant to the situations because they are inundated by special interests or powerful people who commandeer their time. "The squeaky wheel gets the grease" has never been truer when it comes to the government getting things done. This is why it is important for people to rally around their fellow citizens when an injustice occurs. An individual is virtually invisible, but a group has power.

One need only look at our current situation and realize that the issues our country is facing did not happen overnight. They have gradually become larger issues due to the inaction of the people. We allow "officials" to tell us how to live with regard to COVID, yet thousands of people stream across the southern border, and nothing is done. Do those coming into this country illegally not have COVID? Are we not worried about them? The answer is the issue is too large at the border and our government officials only tackle problems that have "solutions" that make them look like they're doing something instead of putting in actual work and making real change. Politicians aren't interested in fixing anything, they only grandstand against the other side, blaming instead of fixing because their ultimate goal is to get reelected, not do anything significant. If they were interested in "fixing" things, they would do it. Instead, they distract us with garbage and keep us fighting amongst ourselves when we should be banding together and finding middle ground and making our elected officials execute those wishes or vote them out of office. But we simply vote for "our side" (there are no sides in government, only the illusion of sides to keep us separated) and perpetuate the problem. Distractions are the downfall of a nation. Modern politicians only seem to be able to achieve mediocrity at best and are actually a detriment at worst. How do we allow this to happen when we have the power to change it? Indolence and indifference, pure and simple.

COVID

It really is amazing that this world has regressed so much that its people have become polarized on what should be a very uniting issue. COVID, if it's the pandemic everyone says it is, should be collectively addressed by all in a "one world" effort. Unfortunately, there are many that stand to profit from this "pandemic". It's very difficult to believe everything we're being told, especially when the people telling us these things are often wrong or deceptive in this and other areas. Perhaps people would be less apt to be defiant if the track record of those "in charge" were a little better. Especially when what they are saying is either sensationalized or wrong. It's especially hard to believe when they are very obviously against whatever certain people say. This is my point, that had everyone worked together from the beginning, we wouldn't be in the mess we're in today.

There are countless millions who have not gotten the vaccine and are fine. There are also other countless millions who did get the vaccine and are also fine. Then there are those select few, relatively speaking, that have had adverse reactions to both getting the vaccine and not getting the vaccine, which begs the question, would those people have been negatively affected either way? Maybe their immune systems couldn't handle either option?

Opinion Double Standards

I find it irritating when someone says I am unable to comment about a certain subject because I am not the person who is experiencing the issue. For example, women claim that men cannot comment on abortion because they are unable to become pregnant. To that I say well, it seems that men CAN become pregnant nowadays? Either way, why is it that I cannot have an opinion or voice my concerns simply because I do not experience the issue firsthand? It would be like saying I can't comment on the plight of women in Afghanistan under Taliban rule because I am not a woman. I have every right to have any comment on anything I choose regardless of how someone else feels about it, people can't wait to shut you down as you haven't experienced what they have, like you can't form an opinion unless you have experienced the issue personally. If people have a problem with me voicing my opinion, then it's their problem, not mine. The real problem is that people feel justified shutting someone else down simply because they don't feel that the other person's opinion has any value. That's just an easy way to shut down an argument to avoid having to justify their ridiculous actions. Also, don't cower to these bullies, look inward to figure out why it is so easy to shut you down. You are as entitled to your opinion as anyone else, be heard. Rise up and ignore those who would attempt to bring, or keep, you down.

A Bit About Women

I touch on this subject later in the book, but if you think about it, while a woman's place may not necessarily be in the home, it certainly does make tactical sense. We joke about it all the time, how if men experienced a menstrual cycle that this world would be noticeably different, to say the least. I couldn't imagine having to live my daily life, working out, getting ready/putting in a full day of work, doing daily chores after work, running errands, taking care of children, etc., all the while battling cramps, emotional unpredictability, other bodily aches, and the worst of all, actively bleeding for two to seven days. It seems unbearable which is why I could see how women usually stayed home while the half of the relationship without multiple physical ailments went to work. I'm sure those who choose to work from home have a much easier time. Just not having to deal with others in person while dealing with menstrual issues would be beneficial. There may be those who have a significant other who works, allowing the woman to stay home and nurse her monthly ailments.

It's commendable that women even get out of bed in the morning during their periods, let alone go to work as police officers, firefighters, military members, etc., very commendable indeed. It almost makes sense to give women time off during that time given the misery I can only imagine they endure. I mean, what a distraction to have to deal with those issues and still care for patients, or design buildings, or wait tables. Those women who choose to work outside of the house definitely deserve some recognition, and possibly some concessions, to offset the sheer agony they endure every month. If COVID has taught us anything it's that not everyone has to come to a workplace to do their job. Perhaps this could be a solution for women who don't absolutely have to leave the house to do their job as long as they have a phone, computer, and internet. Frankly I can't believe it hasn't happened already.

Obviously, there'd have to be some way to verify it as I've heard many stories of women taking advantage of men's ignorance on the subject. Using it as an excuse to get out of certain obligations but I'm sure a system could be implemented where women get a certain amount of "down time" per month to accommodate their cycles. Should they use it unwisely or unscrupulously, then they will just have to suffer through their actual pain. Although, some women experience an easier, and almost non-existent, period, but it would be tough to verify how extreme each woman's period is so a standard time limit would have to be established and other considerations made on a case-by-case basis, if necessary.

I know that men have used the phrase "a woman's place is in the home" in the past, but like I said, it makes a lot of sense if that's what a woman chooses. If they choose to "suck it up and drive on" (i.e., work outside the home) then something should be done to recognize their efforts, or at least make it a little less uncomfortable.

Chapter 9

Quick Hits

- What are people thinking when they speed through a residential area, school zone, etc.? Do they just not realize that children play in those areas? Do they have a false sense of security about their ability to stop should a child run out into the road? Are they unaware that that occurs? I've seen far too many children in my neighborhood just ride their bikes or run out into the street without looking. Speed bumps don't seem to work as I've seen several cars fly over them as well. Not sure what the answer is but I hope someone doesn't have to get hurt before we find it.

- What is it about trends? Do people do these things to impress others? To what end? What if nobody cared? Why does anyone care what anyone else is wearing or driving or using? Are they hoping that people will notice them and therefore get a feeling of satisfaction? Do "trendy" people realize they look silly to most people because it's obvious that they're trying to be trendy? Seems odd to me to care so much about what others think. Who are these others? Maybe they're idiots? It really is strange when you think about it.

- It's amazing how perfectly this country has shown how most people would rather critique or "cancel" others instead of doing something positive to affect change. They feel that "outing" another person for something that person did in high school somehow makes them a crusader for "good". It actually illustrates their extreme laziness, pettiness, and unwillingness to do something positive.

- Some people have no idea how much better they would feel if they would just get enough sleep, eat correctly, and workout a little. It really is about priorities – getting the "quick fix" and suffering later or changing your desires to things better suited for feeling good all the time.

- This country was founded on limiting the overreach of government, yet it seems to have ended up exactly where it didn't want to be. This is mainly due to our leaders emulating King George instead of George Washington.

- If you want people to take care of something, clean something after they use it, or do anything at all, make it easy for them. Set up a system or situation that will be conducive to them performing the task. You want someone to clean up after themselves? Make cleaning supplies readily available. People are leaving something open? Make a sign asking them to close it. BL: people are more apt to do something if you do most of the work. You just have to decide how important it is to you.

- This may be common knowledge, but given the number of jokes made about it, I think it may still be an issue. Are couples still sharing the covers in bed? I don't see how they do it. Yes, it's romantic and nice to cuddle with your significant other but what about when the cuddling is over and it's time to get some serious sleep? A tug-o-war with the covers all night is not conducive to REM sleep. Get separate sets and get some rest.

- No one has the right to waste your time. Don't ever feel guilty for cutting something short if the benefit to both parties is non-existent.

- Why don't those who support tax increases simply pay more taxes than they are required? No one is stopping these "heroes" from cutting a check to the IRS.

- It's funny to see people post things about being tough but humble. Doesn't it defeat the purpose to post that you're humble? It just seems odd to post about how you don't brag about how tough you are but don't mess with you because you're tough?

- Hasn't everyone figured out that in all actuality, diamonds are worthless? There is an abundance of them, yet we pay exorbitant amounts of money to buy them because we're told to. I hate that we do things we know are BS. Notice I said "we" in there?

- I wonder how many people who say they love the city have ever lived in a nice rural town? I think, as with most things, people make choices based on how they think others will perceive them instead of what really makes them happy.

- Who, in their right mind, feels that "yacht" is an acceptable word for a children's television show, book, or game? I've also seen is as a vocabulary word, as if every child will someday encounter a yacht. Seems like a weird choice. It doesn't even have a standard spelling, adding confusion to an already obscure word.

- Speaking of people in their "right mind", who authorized soda and candy machines in schools? What kind of a message are we sending kids? School lunches are already substandard, do we really need to provide them more garbage?

- Does it strike anyone else as odd that we allow companies to advertise on the clothes we already bought, the vehicles we already purchased, etc. It's odd that we would want to wear anything with a company's name on it. Does it mean we support them? I guess? Is it a status symbol? Seems shallow and weak. What about your car? You paid out the nose for a new vehicle and as a bonus, the dealer gets free advertising for a decade or two.

- Always "round up" or donate money at the grocery store checkout. Worst case you lost a couple bucks to a scam. Best case is they help people in your neighborhood. Either way, you put some fuel in your karma gas tank.

- Some say they can't start their day without "x" (not including food/water). I say, grow stronger and find a way. What if you run into a situation where you don't have the thing you need to "start your day"? You'll be at a disadvantage. Try not to "need" anything, it will only hinder your ascension.

Quick Hits

- When people tell great stories about their ancestors, remember that those people were just like you. Live a life your grandchildren will want to tell people about.

- Until we figure out how to fix traffic, find a job that has a different schedule than everyone else. You'll find that your commute, lunch, and down time will be much more enjoyable without an abundance of people slowing your progress.

- Why do we celebrate certain groups each month? In my mind, every month is black history month, or women's history month, etc. The best way to keep a certain group marginalized is to single them out. It's as if it's by design to keep these "groups" from ascending and by making these groups "special" we actually prevent them from achieving true equality.

- Visit so many places that you forget where you've been.

- Does anyone else find it odd that we reward people for not doing bad things? For instance, the military highlights units who don't have DUIs. They commend people for something they aren't supposed to do in the first place. It's like congratulating someone for not murdering. "Hey Joe, good job not killing anyone today!"

- How is it legal for large trucks/vehicles to sit at a height where their headlights are right at eye level for the majority of the vehicles on the road? Shouldn't they at least be oriented down a bit so they don't blind people? It has virtually the same effect as a lower sitting vehicle's brights. Heck, it might be illegal but unless you have definitive proof and the license plate of the offender, you'll never be able to stop it. Speaking of lights, have you ever experienced a clown who has headlights on the rear of their car so they can flash people who they feel are following too close? Maybe it's just in Alaska – there are a lot of things like that.

- If the government truly cared about what we did to the American Indians, they would give them their land back instead of naming things after their tribes as if that somehow makes up for the slaughter. Don't get me wrong, I understand that this country would not be what it is today had our ancestors not been horrible, but the way the government has gone about "making up for it", like using indigenous names for streets, towns, etc. is insulting to American Indians.

- One of the main reasons there is injustice in the world is due to the sheer difficulty to even address and issue. You have to find out who is responsible for the infraction, who governs that individual or organization, gather evidence, present it coherently, find someone who will not only listen but will act, etc. The amount of inaction by those who can affect change is immeasurable. This is especially true if it is going to make "extra" work for them.

- When packing for a trip, whether it be a vacation or a workout, take a mental note of where you packed your things to alleviate having to rifle through your bag to retrieve an item. Then, when you're finished with that item, put it back in the same place for next time.

- With regard to the Harvey Weinstein thing, were the actresses who gave in to him the best or have we been deprived of truly great talent because they refused to succumb to that pig's demands? Think about how many talented people never got a show because they wouldn't give into Weinstein.

- It's odd that this still needs to be said but being offended is a choice. No one can offend you. Also, being offensive is highly subjective. What may "offend" one person may not offend another. That's why it doesn't matter if you allow yourself to be offended because what the "offensive" person is doing may not be offensive to them. This is a free country and, if someone is doing something you don't like, and it's not directly affecting you, your friends and/or family (i.e., you can remove yourself from the situation) then it's none of your business.

- People will attempt to do petty things to you or act petty toward you. In order for those petty things to work (i.e., in order for the petty person to feel satisfied) you have to react to what they did in a negative way. If you do not provide that feedback, then the petty person will not feel satisfied. Don't ever give anyone the satisfaction of knowing that they got to you. This doesn't mean act like they didn't get to you; it means actually not caring about what they say or do.

Chapter 10

Congress

The most frustrating thing about our government is that the legislative branch has the power to do everything necessary to "fix" the nation, yet they screw it up more often than not. This is mainly due to partisan politics getting in the way of common-sense legislation. Their decisions are based on party politics not the needs of the people. Take the spending bills, for instance. They are chock full of funding for people, unfortunately, not all of those people are Americans.

Bills and Resolutions

I talked about bills in my first book and how they are too convoluted, confusing, and bloated for most Americans to read, let alone understand. The most recent spending resolution congress is attempting to pass at the time of this writing is over five thousand pages and has millions of dollars going to foreign countries. Shouldn't we help out the less fortunate? Sure, but maybe we should help our own people first? I mean, what does it say when American children are starving but our legislative branch thinks Pakistani gender programs are more important.

Bills and resolutions should be limited in size and scope. The Constitution was four pages. All other bills should follow this example. They should be short and simple enough for the average American to read and understand and contain one issue each. As it stands, even the members of congress don't have enough time to read the resolutions before they vote on them. Countless senators and representatives admitted openly to not reading H.R. 133 before voting on it.

Unfortunately, the reason these bills and resolutions are so long is that they are touted as one thing (COVID-19 relief) yet contain several different issues, expenses, and/or proposals hidden within them. Instead, congress should present each one of these issues separately so Americans can see exactly what congress has planned for our tax dollars. I believe this is by design so We The People don't notice items that were included in the, so-called, COVID-19 Relief Bill, such as the $100m to Sudan or the $1B to the Smithsonian, or provisions for horseracing and NASCAR.

Here's the link to the resolution if you want to see it for yourself:

https://rules.house.gov/sites/democrats.rules.house.gov/files/BILL

S-116HR133SA-RCP-116-

68.pdf?fbclid=IwAR24sZoGkUFjrmpBWJJOHneQzeNi-

6BN5HlnicDJZEq7BfZ7-JNYlKuQH2Y.

We also need to stop letting those who "predict" what will happen stop common sense legislation. I too often here about the entities like the Congressional Budget Office advising against legislation based on costs not benefit to the people. The military has been hamstrung by this way of thinking for some time, bowing to the bean counters while warfighter training suffers. Our government wastes billions a year, how does the CBO determine on which initiatives to waste money? I'm sure it's way over my head but I do know that no one can predict the future and I also know that saving money isn't always the most important goal, especially when it comes to helping the people of this country. It's not like the government has a stellar track record with being good stewards of The People's money, I think The People would be ok with spending a great deal of money if it helped them in the long run.

Two Party System

How have "we the people" allowed the two-party system to exist as long as it has? Two PRIVATE organizations have absolute control over our country. Can no one see that their only goal is to win and gain/keep power? They have no interest in the people of this country, only to manipulate the people for their own gain and to keep people they can control in office. How is it possible that our government officials are defined by a private corporation's designation? No one working in our government should be shackled to any private organization, let alone be defined by them, yet each congressperson either has a D or an R next to their name. It seems very inappropriate. Do people really think their loyalties lie with the state they represent? They would never defy the party because they need them too much to get reelected which, after all, is their ultimate goal.

What about the hypocrisy? I love it when people say, "do they think we're that stupid?" and the answer is yes, they do, that's why they continue to do it and, to a certain extent, we are because we keep voting in the same offenders. They complain about the horrible behavior of their rival and then later do the exact same thing. It's lunacy. So, in a way, we are too stupid to do anything about it because "we" keep electing the same people. Who are these people, you say? They are the same people who receive millions of dollars from people who want them to do their bidding. It definitely isn't the people but, unfortunately, the people vote for who they are told will represent them the best, even though that candidate has failed to do that very thing for decades! Are they just waiting for the politician to come through on their promise? Are they just giving them another chance, each time hoping the politician makes good on their promises? Or do they blame the other side? "Well, if the other side would have worked with my candidate, they would have kept their promises!" Which is the point. These "public servants" do whatever it takes to stay in office except the one thing we the people need them to do which is look out for us. The solution? Vote all the incumbents out of office. Clean the slate. Vote in new blood. Vote for people that are hungry for justice and not corrupted by the system (yet). Too often we hear these old politicians talk down to us "ignorant" masses because we don't know how "the system" works and we should just trust that they know what's best, and we do!

The "system" does work very well, unfortunately it doesn't work for us. "We" sit idly by while the Pelosis, and McConnells, and Schumers, and Grahams stay in power and look out for their own interests and conduct pseudo-battles against the other side in an attempt to fool us rubes who don't know any better. Don't wait for them to vote in things like term limits, we the people can impose our own term limits with our vote. There are more of us regular citizens than there are billionaires and corporations. We just have to do it.

It really is frustrating that the same people who make the laws either don't have to abide by them or create laws from which only they benefit. Working in one of the three branches of our government should be absolutely exhausting and thankless – it's the only way to guarantee that the person being elected has nothing but the American people's best interests in mind. Take away the reasons that a corrupt person seeks office, and they will cease to do so. Our government officials shouldn't want subsequent terms – it should be that hard.

Insurrection

In January of 2021, a group of idiots "stormed" the capitol and forced "the People's business" to be delayed. Everyone was up in arms about this act because of the meaning they placed upon it. Were they trying to take over the government? If so, why were they escorted by Capitol Police (https://www.youtube.com/watch?v=xfZHk1zu6Vw) or, at least not being engaged by them? Yes, the Capitol Police were outmanned and probably outgunned but why didn't they call for reinforcements? Yes, the five deaths were an absolute tragedy (four of which were protestors, and one who died of natural causes), but for anyone to call this anything other than a slight delay in "the People's business" is being willfully ignorant and overtly disingenuous. Not to mention that there is proof of at least one "left wing" agitator (https://www.politico.com/news/2021/01/14/liberal-activist-charged-capitol-riot-459553) in the midst of the "Trump supporters". It only takes one idiot to instigate something like this, and they did. My point is that people are making more about this than it really is. Congress reconvened later that day after no armed response as most of the suspects not only left on their own, but the crowd dispersed to honor the curfew implemented by the government.

What's my point? More people are upset about an "insurrection" that lasted a couple of hours than they are with our own government attempting to overthrow our own government on a daily basis. Yes, the most recent example of this is Democrats relentlessly pursuing impeachment from the first day of President Trump's term but that isn't the only example of it. Neither side is innocent, they both intentionally sabotage, filibuster, and outright block progress if they think it benefits the other side. Every president has to endure the self-righteous crusaders on the opposite side, "fighting for the people", as if we don't know they're full of it and only doing it to be pugnacious.

Yes, the "rules" they make are perfectly "legal" but only because the same "insurrectionists" vote on the ridiculous rules they make for themselves. This is why they keep getting raises and not term limits. Think how much farther our country would have progressed if the people in Congress actually worked toward a common ground instead of constantly trying to stop each other. This constant blockage of the People's business is exponentially more detrimental than the interruption on January 6th. Anyone who thinks differently is being overly dramatic, which I attribute to this generation wanting so much to be historic that they blow every situation out of proportion to ensure it is solidified in history. What would people do if there was an actual insurrection? They would lose their minds.

Now, do I think what those protestors did was wrong? Of course, it was just as stupid as any other protest. I don't differentiate between protest and riot because neither of them are protected by the First Amendment. As usual, people have twisted the terminology to suit their wants. This is what it says *"peaceably to assemble, and to petition the Government for a redress of grievances"*. This doesn't mean hold disparaging signs, or yell, etc. It means to gather and petition the GOVERNMENT for a redress of grievances. If anything, most of the "rioters" on January

6th were actually exercising this right. They were actually petitioning the government, not looting, burning property, or beating people almost to death. To clarify, the ones that did damage or hurt people were the same as any other thug, but I saw a great deal of people holding flags, walking calmly, praying, etc. Did they go about it the wrong way? Yes. Were they goaded into entering the Capitol by agitators? There's at least one instance where that happened. But for the most part they were saying prayers, laughing, and taking selfies with cops. Conversely, most of the other protests we've seen in recent years do not come close to the definition in the Constitution. I don't think MLK jr. would have approved of most of the protests that have occurred in recent years.

How do we the people allow our government to spend so much? It's really not even most people in congress, it's mostly just those who have been in there a long time and have manipulated the system to work in their favor and keep the status quo, and blame the other party for the debt, deficit, etc. In reality, it's all their fault because they alone have the power to fix it. We the people can only vote them in and out, once they're in there they do whatever they want because it serves those who got them elected, the rich and their political party (which are pretty much synonymous). It really has gotten terrible. These "public servants" get on tv or on the floor of the house/senate and spew their BS and grandstand about the injustices of their political opponents, yet nothing changes. But, as I said, it's our fault because we have the power to vote them out, but we don't. We let them stay where they are and let them continue to make our country weak while China, and other competitors, grow strong. I don't think it's a sinister plan (although it seems that way sometimes, and may be for some, to an extent) but simple laziness, greed, and complacency. They either act, or genuinely feel, that they're serving us, but they aren't. If they truly were "servants of the people", more things would get done, but just like any other government agency, congress is rife with do nothings and narcissists.

Chapter 11

More Presidential Goals

I hear what you're saying, "why you?" Well, Lincoln grew up in squalor and used to float a flatboat loaded with produce and cured meat down the Mississippi. Those are some humble beginnings for a President which means that any of us could potentially do it although, unless the American people come together and abandon the Democrats and Republicans, I'll need to raise about $100 mil to do it.

Also, I have no desire to "go negative" I couldn't care less what the other candidates did or do nor do I care about what they will or won't do for the country. I know that my work ethic, and ambition to make the country better, far surpasses any other candidate. I have no desire to be rich or famous. I have a desire to serve. Some say that's naïve but, without people like me, nothing would get done. I believe in service for many reasons, but most of all I do it because it needs to be done. My mind always comes

back to serving others because there are so many that need help.
As I've said before, the president is the servant of us all and is
actually the least important of us all. For decades we've seen
presidents fail resulting in little to no consequences, how could this
person be more important than anyone else. If I were to gain the
trust of the American people enough to be president, I would not
be haughty but humbled by the gesture.

Global Competition

We don't consider other countries our "enemies" or
"adversaries" anymore, we call them "competitors", it's less
combative that way. The problem is our "competitors" still see us
as adversaries and are actively working to weaken us, and possibly
"destroy" us. Not destroy as in wanton destruction but destroy us
from the inside out, politically, socially, and economically and,
given the current political climate, they just might succeed.

For a long time, the U.S. was the big kid on the block.
Even after Vietnam we were still very much a, if not the,
superpower. As time went on and we focused more and more on

fighting each other. It seems we've lost our edge, or at least our status as the big kid on the block. While we (the Government) were preoccupied with fighting with the other political party, other countries have figured out how to unify their leadership, and flourish. I see Japan growing stronger every day and think that they really have turned themselves around over the decades. Now they're the third-largest economy in the world with no signs of slowing. Pretty good for a country that was part of the Axis and bent on world domination. Maybe they still are but have changed their tactics? Either way, they are doing very well, and I can't remember ever hearing anything about government infighting, or political scandals, etc. It's as if they are focused on making Japan better instead of lining their own pockets?

Another country that seems to be doing well, and getting better by the year, is China. Granted, they manipulate their currency and utilize questionable, and sometimes "illegal" (according to whom?) business practices to ensure their growth but, the point is they are doing what is best for China, not the individual legislator. This allows them to grow at an alarming rate and they will probably overtake the U.S. and rise to the number one slot shortly.

Only recently have we been "fighting back" against countries and entities that are a detriment to our country. Prior to this effort we simply complained about how "unfair" it is while our competitors ignored our whining and grew stronger. Also, our "leaders" seem to think polarizing and dividing us is the best course of action when they should be unifying us. When your "leaders" focus more on alienating half of the country instead of attempting to bring both sides together, you have to question the motives of those "leaders". I sometimes wonder if it's simple incompetence, that our leaders simply don't know how to do their job well and are just fumbling through, faking like they know how to lead.

It's embarrassing how incompetent our legislative branch looks, I can't imagine how the world sees us, this sideshow bickering about petty issues, holding frivolous hearings, lining their pockets while their constituents are homeless in feces ridden streets.

Our country has taken itself for granted for far too long and it's time we start coming together on federal level initiatives at least to ensure we will continue to have a country to take for granted. Yes, there will always be issues on which Americans disagree, but preserving, and improving, the country should never be one of them.

When I become president, I'm going to treat every country as an equal, and as a friend. Now, sometimes friends get in disagreements and have arguments. I don't know a single friend I've ever had that I didn't have some sort of argument with at one time or another. Sometimes friends actually get in fistfights when the other friend steps out of line. If we stepped out of line sometimes you got tightened up a little bit. But that's not to say we couldn't be friends afterwards. I mean look at the 40s. Who would have thought that Germany and Japan would've been such close allies of ours after what happened back then?

People get too dramatic, and they see the world as it was 50 or 100 years ago or even two hundred years ago. It's not the same. We're all here to prosper, we're all here to get better, we all want our country to be the best, so we're cordial to each other. But we hold our own. It should be a secret that we're trying to be better than the next guy, it's a competition, after all, and that's what it should be all about. Healthy competition is good if they're trying to get better. We're all trying to get better. Their success pushes us which pushes them. Sometimes we may do something that's a tad untoward, but we shouldn't do anything too shady, and we can tolerate it if you're doing something that's technically legal but kind of a jerk move. If an ally of ours does something that crosses the line and hurts our people or hurts our country then yes, we're going to retaliate, or at least discuss it and figure out what the deal is and go from there. But no country is our "enemy" and anybody that says that doesn't understand people or how the world works. Now, people may consider us their enemy, and that's on them, that's their problem, but as far as we're concerned everybody gets a fair shake and tightened up as necessary.

Social Security vs. Social Programs

I don't claim to be an expert but, from everything I've read about Social Security, it's hanging on by a very thin thread. Due to more people retiring than paying in (and longer life spans) SS is not sustainable. As president, I will do whatever I can to stop broken systems like SS that have plagued this nation for decades. We have proven that we can generate funds out of "thin air" (seemingly) so I think we can come up with something to fix SS. Off the top of my head, we immediately stop deducting from everyone at the time of this effort and generate funds elsewhere to cover those who have already reached the "retirement" age. We should also refund the money to those who choose that option and keep the rest to accrue interest but not take any more from anyone.

Another option would be to overhaul it and find a better way to invest the money to ensure a better rate of return. This could be done by the government, but a better option would be to hire a successful investment firm and give Americans the option to invest with the "government" (through a private, successful, firm) or keep the money to invest for themselves. A solely government-run program is rarely a good option, so we need more private, successful, businesses involved to ensure prosperity.

Now, on the other hand if you are receiving anything from the government there must be a system in place to repay that debt. Simply giving "free money" to anyone is bad business and will only result in more debt – or higher taxes. Neither of these are optimal unless the government is getting something for their money. The government doesn't owe anyone anything except safety, interstate infrastructure, and other things you might not be able to procure on your own. Everything else should be provided by state/local governments or procured yourself.

Now, there is something to be said about providing people with basic survival needs but it isn't sustainable without some kind of payback method. If you are unable to procure your own food, water, and/or shelter then there should be a program to help but in return you should have to provide some sort of service. Otherwise, other taxpayers, who are taking care of themselves, are expected to take care of you as well. It's not fair to those who are self-sustaining to pay for others who are not. This is where the "payback" services could help. Whatever talent the person receiving the government support has can be used to help others. This talent may be as simple as sweeping floors or picking up garbage, but it will help those whose taxes are being used to help.

Another option would be to record the debt and have the receiver pay it back when they get on their feet. However, this could take an exorbitant amount of time and almost defeats the purpose of providing these services without cost unless the receiver becomes very successful. Perhaps a small payment each month to assist in the cost of the services? Although, I don't know if that would be better than the citizen performing an actual service for their community. Either way, if you receive assistance from the government, it means you are receiving assistance from your fellow citizens, and it isn't fair to them that they must pay for themselves and you.

Privatization

Speaking of assistance from the government, I will also begin an initiative to make it lucrative for big businesses to take over government programs like welfare, social security, department of education, FDA, FAA, etc. These corporations will not have full control, as there will be government oversight from a small agency comprised of personnel with varying viewpoints who all have equal voting rights on how things should progress. This will ensure no partisan bias is influential in the decisions being made. The corporations will run their respective agencies as they would their own corporation to reduce waste and improve efficiency. We already use private corporations to run some of our government programs. TRICARE, for instance, is subcontracted to several different companies throughout the U.S. Each "region" operates separately from the others and changes subcontractors every couple of years. I think privatizing more government agencies, with a very small government oversight office, would lower costs, eliminate fraud, waste, and abuse, and ultimately provide a better "product" for the customer...us.

The plan is to provide tax incentives for those companies that take over the operation of a government program or division. For instance, Google will receive a tax break, or some other government incentive to take over the department of education. A small, diverse, federal agency will provide oversight, but Google would run day-to-day operation of the department. Government agencies are notoriously run poorly, and I believe that the right leadership, and vision, could produce excellent results. While government leaders have tried to appoint successful people, the infrastructure is to blame for the failings. Yes, a good leader should be able to motivate the people who work for them to succeed but the innerworkings of government agencies squash any hope of innovation or incentive to lean forward and go above and beyond.

Politics also plays a large role in the substandard practices of government agencies. Every four to eight years a different "leader" is appointed to these agencies based on their political affiliation which means that the whole system has to be overhauled to fit the new party's agenda. If private corporations ran federal programs, there would be no change in the innerworkings of the departments as they would have no political ties.

The Justice System

The best option for everyone (except judges and lawyers) is to avoid the justice system altogether. It has become a cesspool of corruption, indolence, and complacency and is only advantageous to those with money. Those of us who must use it are either left paying obscene amounts of money to a person who can't guarantee success or spending an exorbitant amount of time conducting research and drafting paperwork on our own.

It's absolute lunacy that a person can pay a lawyer tens, sometimes hundreds, of thousands of dollars and still lose. How is that right? The rules of the justice system are so convoluted that it's nearly impossible for a "layman" to successfully navigate it. As president I would work with lawmakers to standardize and simplify the justice system. I would make it so judges and lawyers don't profit from the ignorance and/or inability of a regular citizen just trying to receive justice. A person may have presented a valid, and legal, argument but if they didn't file the proper paperwork or failed to say a very specific thing, etc. then they lose the case. We talk about universal health care, free college, etc. why not the legal system? Heck, you can't even file a complaint without paying a filing fee, I mean, what is the purpose of the fee?! Aren't the people already being paid to process paperwork like this? Where does the money go? How is it being used? I'm told it's to buy computers or paper, etc. But shouldn't the state and/or federal government be paying for those items? Why does a citizen have to pay for a right granted to them by the constitution? Because "We The People" have allowed them to. We need to demand "Universal Legal Care" so normal people aren't continually raked over the coals by people who are trained to manipulate.

The legal system has become bastardized just like everything else. It is designed to make lawyers money by having frivolous hearings, pre-trial hearings, omnibus hearings, calendar calls, etc. The system seems set up to get the defendant and the plaintiff in the courtroom as much as possible as if to enable the lawyers to charge more fees? Why aren't all those things done in one day or via email? The legal system needs to be revamped and streamlined. There is too much bureaucracy and wasted time. When I worked for the state and had to go to court for a case, half the time the lawyers weren't ready and we had to reschedule immediately. We're talking about parents who have lost their children and the lawyers were ill prepared to talk about the case and the rescheduled hearing would not be in a day or so but weeks later. To a judge or lawyer this may not mean anything, but to a parent a day is too much let alone weeks! I used to feel so bad for the parents. Some may have deserved to have their child taken from them, but they also deserved to be heard. Not all of them were guilty and to delay the reunion of a family because a lawyer is ill prepared is unforgiveable, yet it happened all the time. The saddest part is the incompetence was not only allowed but seemed to be fine to the judge. The fact is that they were all lawyers at one time and rig the system in their favor, not the people they are meant to serve.

One last thing about lawyers is how they allow for "loopholes" in the law to win cases. It's appalling how everything else could be right but one small aspect is incorrect or not according to a specific law or procedure and either the criminal walks or the person in the right loses the case. Common sense doesn't seem to be entertained in a courtroom as long as the proper procedures are followed. Doesn't seem right.

Initiatives

This section is dedicated to things I'd like to see implemented during my presidency. They may seem farfetched but so did the abolition of slavery and women's rights at one time. The only limitations we have are those we allow.

Citizens born with lethal conditions

For instance, there are many people born with afflictions that the majority of us never have to endure. There are also children who develop afflictions that are out of anyone's control. I believe these afflictions should be taken care of by a government fund specifically for that purpose. This could be funded by donations, an alternate funding stream, or possibly even taxes but a child shouldn't have to suffer due to something no one could control. Obviously, we would have to determine the severity of these afflictions to determine who "needs" care. I believe all children need help, but I don't think it's fair that a non-lethal, non-debilitating, or "non-costly" affliction should be taken care of by the government. I put "non-costly" in parenthesis because that can be relative to the family's financial situation so those cases will be taken case-by-case. There are non-lethal afflictions that can be costly to a family, and I don't think there is anything wrong with helping those people. This will need to be well defined to avoid abuse. Stipulations must be put in place to ensure corruption doesn't occur in the future.

Feminine "Issues"

In the same vein as "things people can't control", I think it's unfair that a woman should have to pay for her feminine hygiene products. This may seem out of left field but, after having lived in a house full of women, I have developed a deep sense of empathy for what women go through each month. It's downright unfair they have to endure such tribulations regularly and any help we can give them might ease that burden, at least a little. Offering free feminine hygiene products is a very logical step to help those who had no choice in which gender they would be and the inherent trials that accompany it.

Holidays

Another change I would make would be for all federal holidays to be observed on Fridays (or Thursdays if I am able to implement a 4-day work week). Additionally, I would make the following Monday a work holiday to give everyone a four- or five-day weekend, depending on the work schedule we have at the time.

Alternate Work Locations

Due to the lessons we've learned from COVID-19 regarding the ability for most Americans to telework, I would implement alternate work locations. This means if you don't absolutely have to be at work to do your job, you can work from anywhere, provided you have adequate telephone and email service.

If COVID-19 is still a threat, for those personnel who must come into work, we will reconfigure workspaces to accommodate social distancing and/or create isolated work areas. We could do this by building up cubicles or putting acrylic glass around each workstation. Obviously, this wouldn't work for all federal positions, but we will implement this course of action wherever feasible.

Teleworking would also alleviate a person's need to highlight that they came in early, stayed late, worked the weekend, etc. I find it odd that people brag about these things. Are they trying to impress? It always seems to have the opposite effect, especially if the person's co-workers are doing comparable work. Are the people who work long hours and weekends wasting time during normal work hours or are they trying to get ahead? If it's the latter, then that hard work will get noticed naturally without them highlighting their efforts. The results will show that they put in the extra work for the betterment of the company/mission/etc. but some are so insecure, or guilty, that they feel the need to tell everyone about their "extra effort". This usually results in co-workers resenting the person for being a "spotlighter" and the boss thinking they are just being obsequious. It's always better to be a "silent professional" for their reward is exponentially greater than the "spotlighter". It shows that you have a higher purpose than just getting noticed and will speak volumes about your character. But the trick is not to do it for this reason either. Adopting a selfless attitude and the satisfaction of accomplishing your goals will be rewarding enough, everything else is extra.

Now, if you are specifically asked through direct feedback, a performance report, etc., then you must fight the urge to be humble for this is an acceptable time to highlight your hard work.

Supervisors expect you to forgo your humility and talk openly about your efforts so they can properly assess, and possibly reward, you for the good you've done for the unit/team/business.

The time for recognition will come naturally, don't force it or you will look like that is your only reason for doing the work. If that is the case then you may want to find a different line of work, one that will allow you to be fulfilled by the effort, not the appreciation.

Voting

Why is it so hard to believe that the U.S. voting is flawed? Our elections have been controlled by people with money for centuries. Also, it is run by people, meaning not entirely automated, and extremely "loose" (a term we used in the military to describe a person or persons who weren't squared away). There is so much potential (and confirmed proof) that the system is affected by social media, human error, human meddling, etc. that it is laughable to think it's infallible. Also, the U.S. has been meddling in other countries' elections for decades, how could we possibly think ours is immune? China and Russia need only hire a company to flood social media with propaganda supporting the side they think will be most malleable to them.

The way we vote in this country must be revamped and streamlined. There is too much room for error and those errors matter in tight races. How are we still using pen and ink to cast votes, relying on humans to count those votes, not associating each vote with a social security number, and allowing "mail-in" ballots? I'm not talking about absentee ballots that people request and are then sent, I'm talking about hundreds of thousands of unsolicited

ballots mailed out (sometimes in duplicate and triplicate) to people

that may or may not be receiving them. How do we guarantee that

the person sending in the ballot is the person on the ballot? The

truth is there is no way to be sure and this is by design, this allows

for manipulation of the results. It's lunacy that we use the voting

methods in place today. It's also crazy that each state has its own

process. I am a firm believer in State's rights but when it comes to

a federal issue that affects the entire country, the process should be

standardized. The federal government must create a web site

where a person logs in, enters their social security number, and

votes. It can be a secure server to which only a few trusted agents

have access. A person would be able to log in at any time and

check the status of their vote to ensure it was cast for the

candidates they chose. The voting could be open for a week before

election day to allow for the servers to handle the traffic. Then, on

election day, at 11:59 pm Hawaii Standard Time, you'll have a

definitive answer regarding the election. If the states wanted to

maintain control, they would be provided a similar system strictly for their state, but it would be overseen and checked by a federal agency.

I believe the voting system we currently have is by design and meant to allow for manipulation and ambiguity to allow for "tweaking" as deemed necessary by whoever has the means. I know, this sounds far-fetched and "tin foil hat"-ish but, as I said, the U.S. has been controlling elections in other countries for years, why is it so hard to believe that we would control our own?

Worldwide Investing

We occupy a lot of space in this world but how much of it do we actually own? How much of it can we use to generate income? Very little, if any. That doesn't seem like something "we" do. I'd like to change that. I would like to invest in real estate around the globe and actually own it and develop it to not only generate income for the U.S. but help those less fortunate to prosper. Just think if we could build up an impoverished part of the world and make it profitable? Or buy real estate here in the U.S. and run it like a business. I'm sure there's a law or rule against this but why? Why rely on the people to fully fund the government?

Another option would be to invest in a hedge fund, or hire a hedge fund manager to invest our money, etc. Again, I'm sure there are "rules" or "laws" against it but those can be changed. Why not put our money to work for us instead of it being wasted by the government? How much better for the government to be self-sustaining and not need tax money to operate? People forget that the income tax hasn't always been around. Although it started during the Civil War, it wasn't official until 1913 when our "leaders" all voted for the 16th amendment. They tried it before in 1894 but the Supreme Court struck it down as unconstitutional, however just like all horrible ideas, the legislative branch kept it alive, acted autonomously, and ratified the 16th amendment.

It's typical, lazy, progressive thinking that we can tax our way out of debt, relying on others to help instead of helping ourselves. The government expects Americans to do this, yet they won't. It's too hard to draft legislation or too far above them to figure out the details. They would rather stay with the same status quo and not balance the budget, go further in debt, and betray their constituents. If there are laws against it, change the laws. If there is an amendment preventing this action, repeal it. Unfortunately, our current "leaders" lack the proper courage and drive to do what's necessary for the good of the country.

Privacy

Due to invasive tech companies, public and private cameras (security, traffic, etc.), and everyone having the ability to record you at any moment, it seems like a person's privacy is rapidly eroding. If a person is in a public place, they should instinctively know that they could be observed, recorded, and scrutinized at all times. However, if a person is in a "private" place, whatever that may be, their privacy should be aggressively guaranteed. While I think this is mostly prevalent in our society, I think it should include electronic devices and, if that privacy is violated, the punishment must be so severe that it isn't worth the trouble of doing it in the first place.

A person should be afforded the right to privacy whenever they want when in their private residence. The only exception to this rule would be if the person is suspected of a crime but, even then, the stipulations must be very clear and relatively stringent as to not erroneously target the wrong person. The point is unless you're in your own home, expect to be watched by the world, and act accordingly. If you are home alone then your privacy should be as protected as your life. No one other than law enforcement should be able to monitor a person in their home. People are exposed enough and should have a safe haven from any and all prying eyes and ears.

Money

Why does the federal government continue to issue pennies and nickels? They lose about $69-85m dollars a year making pennies and the nickel (5¢) costs 7¢ each which costs us another $33m. So, why do we still do it? Yes, we make up the deficit with dimes and nickels but, wouldn't it be more responsible to cease production of the penny and nickel and put the extra $100m to some good use? I've heard it's to keep prices low but is it?

Wouldn't it be easier to just round up anyway? A lot of stores have been asking if we want to round up to help the local food bank, or COVID relief, etc., why not implement that as a way for the government to make some extra money? Get rid of the penny and nickel and mandate that all purchases will be rounded up to the nearest dollar and that extra change will be given to the government? I'm sure that would add up to a pretty good chunk of change. Then we could do away with the income tax altogether. I think people would gladly accept paying a little more for each item for the ease of balancing their budget and not having their paycheck taxed.

Speaking of money, I would ensure that the military's financial process is streamlined. The bureaucratic red tape that exists in the military's contracting world is abhorrent, often to the point whereby the time an item is sourced, built, and shipped, it is obsolete or no longer needed. Pieces of equipment arrive at units after something far better has been created. Buildings are erected so slowly that thousands of training hours are wasted waiting for it to be completed. Heck, there have been whole military bases constructed that have immediately been abandoned due to shifting priorities.

This isn't always the case though. In special operations, for the most part, funds are allocated, kit is purchased, and buildings are erected in a timely manner because they use common sense and aren't fully controlled by the "bean counters". Usually, these initiatives have the backing of a high-ranking officer who can expedite the effort but that begs the question, why can't all the projects be expedited if it just takes a few high-ranking officers to authorize it? Things can happen quickly in the military, if it's important enough to the person making the decisions. What they don't realize is that other units are trying to do their mission but don't have the luxury of a general helping them, so they plod along, doing their mission with substandard equipment.

Yes, the "bean counters" will call me naïve and say that "there is only so much money to go around" and "we must prioritize what we get" but to that I say ask for more. Make the effort to highlight the needs of those you serve. "Bean counters" either don't know, or don't care what happens on the "front lines" and it shows.

When I say "bean counters" I'm not talking about the unit level comptrollers, I'm talking about higher level personnel who fancy themselves more important than the warfighter because they hold the "purse strings". I've seen these people in budget meetings scoff and deny initiatives because they don't fully understand the gravity if the initiatives aren't funded. I've seen warfighters denied training and equipment in order to fund the politically attractive effort, efforts that usually cost way too much money for what their worth and will, potentially, prepare the command for the future, although the chances of it actually coming to fruition, let alone helping is 50/50. It's usually some "leader's" vision of the future that they won't be around to see implemented because they will have moved on to another job before the initiative is completed, if at all. What can happen is the "champion" of the effort is assigned somewhere else and the initiative is left to atrophy because no one who cares is there to see it through.

Military

There are certain things that I would change regarding how the president uses the military. I don't mean defending the nation, armed conflict, etc., I'm talking about how each presidential candidate uses the military for political purposes. Promises to draw down troops in country "x", commitment of troops to effort "y", etc. I'm sure someone has an explanation about why we telegraph troop movements, draw downs, etc. but I don't think it's valid. No one has the right to know what we're doing with our troop besides the troops and their chain of command. While the American people think it is our right to know everything that goes on with the military, they are sorely mistaken. They only need to know that, hopefully, the government is using the military in a manner that is beneficial to the U.S., whatever that may be. Telegraphing troop movements or advertising strategies only allows the enemy to know what we're doing. Perhaps it's a ploy or misdirection to take the focus off some other operation but I firmly believe that we give away too much. How much do we know about China and their military exploits? What about Russia? The average person only knows what is found out because those two entities divulge next to nothing.

Do our leaders have a false sense of security, or a true one? It's hard to say, but when I see press conferences where reporters ask the press secretary if it's true that the president is going to draw down troops to a certain number in a certain area, it seems like we're putting the lives of those deployed in danger.

If I were in charge, most things we do regarding combat deployments would at least be "Controlled Classified Information" and possibly "Confidential" or "Secret". The less our "competitors" know about us the better. This not only allows us plausible deniability but a certain degree of mystery to keep our "competitors" on their heels.

IRS

Do we really need the IRS? Do we need an organization that refuses to handle in person problems until they feel it's necessary and then do so with invasive audits? They have the manpower and time to send everyone who received a stimulus payment a letter in the mail (envelope, paper, stamp, etc.) but they can't answer questions?

253

We wouldn't need the IRS if we implemented the initiatives I mention elsewhere in this book. Taxes should be straightforward with no loopholes or breaks. Just flat taxes that are easy to pay and easy to track. A certain percentage should be taken out of each paycheck to alleviate the need for anyone to have to "do their taxes" each year. I would also eliminate things like capital gains taxes, etc. We need to find a way for the government to earn money, not just "make" it from its citizens.

A good way to "earn" money is to increase taxes on "nice to have" items. Citizens would get behind a law that let them keep more of their money and only be taxed if they chose to buy certain items. I'm sure there would be come controversy on what is deemed "necessary" but I'm sure we could boil it down and figure it out. Some people in our current government are both lazy and shady so they just go with what's easiest and what will most benefit them, not necessarily what's best for the American people. I get it, we need taxes for interstate issues, etc. but it just seems like the easy way out. Let elected officials earn that hefty paycheck and actually do something for us, not just keep the status quo, AKA: the path of least resistance.

For those who say, "you just don't understand" or "well, that's not how it works", are no better than those who can't figure out workable solutions that serve the people. Yes, that's the way the "system" works now because those "in power" have made it that way. There is nothing stopping them from changing they system, they are literally the only ones who can change the system. Unfortunately, changing the current system won't benefit them and their donors so it doesn't get done. The only way to fix this problem is to vote everyone out and not vote for either political party. Yes, there will be growing pains but maybe that's what this country needs, a shake up, some free thinkers who aren't bogged down by "the way it's always been" and are free to make changes that make sense for everyone, not just those "in power". Alas, this country is terrible at coming together and only really does so when there's a major tragedy, which is also a tragedy. If only we could figure out how to put our stupid differences (perpetuated by the political parties) aside and come together for the issues that actually affect all of us.

Modification of the Electoral College

One of the biggest issues people have with the electoral college is that big cities don't normally vote the way the rest of the state does. If it weren't for those big cities, the state would usually vote for someone else. So, why don't the cities separate like Washington D.C., become their own entity, and have their own electoral votes? They could operate as D.C. does thereby allowing the rest of the state to not be influenced (negatively or positively) by the tremendous populations of their biggest cities. It seems like a fair trade-off, and it would ultimately serve both sides or, at least make it fair in that most left leaning people seem to congregate to the major cities whereas center-right leaning people seem to spread out and want more individual space. Although, all this could be moot if we could find a candidate that didn't alienate half the country. Unfortunately, as long as we have two major parties, who wield far too much power and influence, we are stuck with this system.

The Future of the U.S.

The way things are going in the U.S. today it almost seems like someone (read: many somones) is intentionally distracting the citizens of the U.S. in order to weaken us. Our borders are porous, we aren't very focused on national security, we have a very odd foreign policy, and are constantly distracted with non-issues.

The U.S. seems to have lost focus on staying a superpower and is, instead, focused on ensuring no one ever experiences any adversity or hardship at the expensive of the future of the Nation. Meanwhile, China and Russia are expanding their empires, kind of overtly, while we continue to give up on that which we've spent blood and treasure. For instance, at the time of this writing, the U.S. has pulled completely out of Afghanistan almost intentionally to make room for China to move in to continue its mining, among other, operations. They have also gradually made a significant presence in Africa, an untapped resource, another resource that we can't figure out. We're adequate at occupying other regions and looking for terrorists but we are terrible at nation building and getting a return on our investment. Well, I say "we" but really I mean the government, which has become a mechanism for businesses to become stronger while the country grows weaker. Not that I'm against business, on the contrary, I believe business is the answer but only if used properly. Our government continues to help businesses yet doesn't do anything for the people of the country. But I digress, unless we (the government) start getting in the game, and expanding OUR empire, we're going to cease being a superpower and more of a pawn (not that we haven't become that already).

The scary thing about what I mentioned above is that half of the country is on board with what is happening. They've wanted the U.S. to be knocked down a few pegs due to the history of the nation. According to them, the U.S. deserves the strife it's experiencing. Too many white men, not enough of, literally, anything else. Well, why does the U.S. have to grow weaker for those "oppressed" to grow stronger? I'm all about equality and diversity but not at the cost of our country's basic values – life, liberty, and the pursuit of happiness. This country has always been about freedom and prosperity, but neither one of these come easily or without some cost. Unfortunately, we have become this beacon of light for everyone yet failed to remind everyone how we got here. Instead, we have leaders bowing to the demands of an entitled populace who demand everything be given to them for free while they do nothing to earn it. This briefs really well but, beyond that, it doesn't make sense. The country was forged on the blood, sweat, and tears of those willing to work for it. In order for this country to stay great it must be inhabited by people who share this same work ethic. Unfortunately, those looking for a free ride are increasing, and it is mainly due to some people in our government sharing these views. It doesn't matter to them that there are those of us who must pay more and work harder to support those who want these free things, they just want votes and votes come from people, people who receive things from those candidates.

The bottom line, it's futile to reason with those who seem like they're against the country because that's exactly what they are. They think the policies that are a detriment to the thriving of this country are a good thing and that "we" (our country) has never been good or right, aside from the incidences that fit their agenda. I don't understand why anyone would want to hurt the very place that has made them who they are. Some citizens of the U.S. will admit how they gained their prosperity, they simply want to condemn the very system that provided it.

Fortunately, right now we are, for the most part, doing pretty well. Maintaining the status quo as much as possible. Bettering our own lives as much as possible. All the while the U.S. is taken down, piece by piece, by some in the government. It doesn't affect us, too much, right now but what about the future? What about future generations? I guarantee that China will be here long after we're (the U.S.) is gone if we don't do something now. I get a kick out of the people who fight for the climate but not the actual country. China couldn't care less about the environment and are untouchable. China does what it wants, when it wants, and has help from Russia and Iran. Meanwhile we bow down to every single thing that may make our politicians look bad. You can only be the benevolent giant for so long before the other giants, who couldn't care less about benevolence, grow stronger and take you out.

Epilogue

As with the first TILT, I cover many subjects in this book. I do this because I feel that there are many things that people aren't exposed to in their life and if I can come up with as many things as possible, maybe one or more of them will help others. My goal with these books (and anything I do, really) is to help people. It's not to get recognition, or fame, or money but because I feel that if you have the means, power, wherewithal to do something, you should. If I don't then who will? Maybe someone else will, which would be great as that would provide more resources to help others.

So, as always, if you need something or have a question about anything, shoot me an email and I will do what I can to help. Jarrod@tryitlikethis.net.

You may not do everything you want in life, but

do everything you can.

About the Author

Jarrod Welsh

Jarrod Welsh retired from the US Air Force after ~24 years of service, over half being with special operations. Following his retirement he worked in Child Protection for two years and is currently a military contractor. He and his wife also write children's books and have four children.

Twitter: @TryItLikeThis
IG: @jarrod_TryItLikeThis
FB: @TryItLikeThis
Web: tryitlikethis.net

<u>Notes</u>

Notes

Notes

Notes

Notes